Entrepreneurship 101:
Start a Business
A Winery Case Study

Stuart L. Scott

Moscow, Idaho

i

Entrepreneurship 101:
Start a Business
A Winery Case Study

Published by
Stuart L. Scott
112 S. Main St.
Moscow, Idaho

Copyright Stuart L. Scott, 2019

Printed by Amazon

ISBN: 978-1-7322468-4-3

Cover Design by Tania Suarez Mendoza

Acknowledgements

Thanks to the people who were willing to teach me; Thomas Kruse, who taught me winemaking; Phil Olson, who taught me about business and my editor, Gordon Long, who taught me to organize a book.

Contents

xi

Foreword

"Stu Scott is not one to waste steps, mince words or treat his winery as a hobby. In fact, he and his wife Sue live above their downtown business. He annually wins awards at the Los Angeles County Fair and routinely receives praise from Wine Press Northwest, typically in our "Best Buy!" section. Remarkably, he doesn't sell a bottle in his production of 2,000 cases for more than $20. But it helps to explain why he is our 2007 Idaho Winery of the Year."

— Wine Press Northwest Magazine, Spring 2007 Issue

Preface

Why did I write this book? I wrote it because I believe human knowledge to be a cumulative affair. When I started my winery in 1983, I had enough winemaking skill to win a commercial award in my rookie year. But, as you'll learn in this book, I didn't start out with the skills or knowledge to be a success in the wine business. I now realize how much I learned about business during the past twenty-nine years as a professional winemaker.

While reading this book, please remember that the rules for any business are ever changing. You should verify that the advice and facts I give are current. Prices and costs also change, so concentrate on the rationales and reasons that I present rather than just the numbers in my examples.

Thanks to my winemaking mentor Tom Kruse, who showed me the valuable concepts of adapting everyday items, such as food-grade plastic drums and hose, to winery use. He taught me to never cheat or skimp on the really important things and to know the difference between what was necessary and what was just nice. Most of all, Tom Kruse showed me how to keep the enjoyment in my winery. Thanks, Tom. Or, as Tom would say, "Ha, Ha, Ha, what?"

* * *

As my book goes into its third printing, I've continued to listen and learn from readers. My book is about business, because the lessons and information presented are not specific to the wine trade. To illustrate, take your business idea, whatever it might be, and insert your terminology in place of my wine lingo. I have added a subheading at each chapter that highlights the "General Business Points" contained there. You'll find personnel, production space/time, continuity of supply, and selling to multilevel markets are still your issues, whatever you are making or doing. Throughout this sharing experience, I will stress different aspects of how being a problem solver—both for your customers and within your own business—can be accomplished. My goal is that you find value in what I've learned. My hope is that you are as successful as I have been and have as much fun as I've had.

Happy trails. Oh, and try to avoid any plans that start or end with "What could possibly go wrong?"

Stu Scott

1. My Mid-Life Crisis and the Winery Dream

General business points:
- **Why start a business?**
- **The basics of business**

The Basics of My Industry—Life Lessons

In 1981, I left my home in one of California's many wine regions and arrived in Moscow—home of the University of Idaho. The prime reason for this move was to free my wife from the work force and allow her to be home with our four children.

Why, oh Why?

Upon landing in Idaho, I suffered my first mid-life crisis due to the death of my father. His passing caused me to re-evaluate my own life. I decided I wanted more satisfaction out of life and I was willing to make trade-offs and changes to achieve that goal. I was willing to make less money while having more fun, a better family life, and more free time. In California, as a hobbyist, I made wine and planted my own two-acre vineyard. I loved the lifestyle that I saw among the small wineries in my neighborhood and found satisfaction in making and sharing my wines. The long-term plan was to create a viable business that would allow me to enjoy an early retirement from the government at age fifty, some fifteen years in the distance.

My wife, Sue, was the creative force that picked the winery name, chose our logo design, and named one of our most successful products, a wine known as Hog Heaven Red. Best of all, she could spell and proofread! I consulted her at every opportunity. As an added bonus, Sue agreed to do the books for the business. She enrolled in an adult education bookkeeping

1

class to gain the minimum skill level needed. I loved Sue when I married her and loved her even more as we shared the new adventure of the winery.

Learning the Basics of the Industry

I had to learn the rules of the wine game. What licenses were required? Where, how, and to whom could I sell my wine? How much wine could I or should I make? Are my hobbyist wines of commercial quality? Should I become a corporation or be a sole proprietor? What about product liability and liquor liability insurance? What are the labeling rules for wines? Where do I find suppliers for grapes, bottles, corks, and labels? What would it cost me to start my business?

I started my quest by approaching Tom Kruse and asking if he would become my paid consultant to help me get the winery off the ground. He agreed. Next, I learned where to find the federal and state rules. I found trade journals that helped with locating goods and services I would need. I called on friends who had expertise I lacked and recruited them as consultants.

What I Learned About My Intended Industry

There are four levels of licensing and permits required: federal, state, county, and city. Owning only some of the necessary winemaking hardware. I found sources for additional fermenters, barrels, a bottle filler machine, and a better corker. I evaluated options on new equipment that was also necessary for commercial operations, and located instruments for filtering and labeling bottles. I learned the rules pertaining to wine labels and regulations concerning wine sales and distribution. After all this research, I was finally ready to embark on my quest. Going in, I knew that producing good wine was just the price of admission to this club I hoped to join.

Life Lessons and the Business

I'll start you out with six of my life's lessons:

- Don't screw up a perfectly good hobby by trying to make money at it

2

- Friends judge us and our works by a different standard than strangers do
- In a small business, you are the janitor, dishwasher, and last minute substitute worker
- Hope for the best but plan for the worst—things will go wrong
- Be aware of what you don't know
- Keep it simple—don't be seduced by initial success

Conclusions

To paraphrase Donald Rumsfeld, whom I once helped guard, "We don't know what we don't know." Every type of business endeavor will have its own set of unique rules, besides the more general rules of the business world. The unique rules may come from the EPA or some level of federal, state or local government. To be a success and avoid unintended problems, you must research the rules pertaining to your intended business and its greater industry.

Why start a business? The answer, from my days as a psychology grad student, comes from Maslow's 'hierarchy of needs' theory. Once we have met our primary, survival needs: food, shelter, clothing, then we strive to obtain non-material needs: love, recognition, self-satisfaction. I reduced all of the 'WHY' to this; when we're dead, we're dead for a hell of a long time, so try it—do it—now. Don't grow old simply to hold hands with the clock and your regrets.

2. Is Your Product Good Enough?
Don't ask Mom

General business points:
- **Quality of your product**
- **Choosing your market category**

If your wife or girlfriend asks you, "Does this dress make my rear end look fat?" is she apt to get an honest answer? So, imagine asking Mom or Uncle Harry, "Is my product any good?" How honest do you anticipate their answer to be if they love you, or at least have forgiven you for all the crummy things you did as a kid?

Research Strategies

If you want to know if your wine is of commercial quality, ask strangers and industry professionals. Approach industry professionals: in my case, distributors, restauranteurs, and wine shop owners. These are the people that will be asking the public to buy your wines. Their opinion is of greater importance than Mom's.

The local Moscow wine shop put me in touch with a wine distributor's representative who evaluated my wine and suggested realistic price ranges. Luckily, he found my wine to be "of good commercial quality" and something he could sell.

Picking the Right Part of the Market

Are you going to compete in the market place based on price, quality or a mid-point between the two that can be called value? The choice you make will suggest a general price point. Then do market research within your target market to find the best, most profitable price for your product.

I learned that there are four general categories of wines: jug wines, fighting varietals, premium wines, and ultra-premium wines. Price categories are generally linked to wine quality but each group will also have visual clues. As the wines become better, from jug wine to ultra-premiums, each category uses progressively more expensive grapes and packaging.

Jug wines

Usually packaged in larger bottles, 1.5 liter, half-gallon, gallon, or in boxes. There is no vintage dating or indication of the type of grapes used shown on the package. Jug wines compete based on price.

Fighting varietals

Not generally packaged in gallon or half-gallon bottles. We find them in 750 ml, 1.5 liter or boxed in these corresponding sizes. The package will show the type of grape or grapes used in the wine and the most favorable legal information concerning the origin of the fruit.

In the wine business, labeling laws tightly regulate what can be said about origin of the fruit and actual producer of the wine. (I suspect other industries have similar labeling rules.) Fighting varietals compete on value for admittedly lower-priced wines.

Premium wines

Almost always sold in 750 ml bottles. Usually they have enhanced label details, including the type(s) of grapes used, a vintage date and advantageous labeling about the fruit source: appellation, state and perhaps vineyard. They compete on both price and quality, striving to be the best value.

Ultra-premium wines

Share the general packaging characteristics of premium wines, but emphasize the prestige of the producer or appellation. They will also often use more expensive packaging such as heavier or embossed bottles and fancier labels. Without intending to 'damn them with faint praise,' ultra-premium wines will maximize the use of show-biz to pump up their price. Usually the added price for an ultra-premium is justified but not always. They compete solely on the basis of quality.

Business Plan

There are many books that describe in detail what goes into a *business plan*. A business plan will be a written outline of where you want to go and how you plan to get there. The business plan will also be the vehicle for presenting your dream to the bank, investors or other financing source. You start with:

Executive summary: a snapshot of your business

- Market analysis – research on your industry, market and competitors
- Organization and management – your business and management structure
- Service or product – the products or services you're offering
- Marketing and sales – how you'll market your business and your sales strategy
- Funding request – how much money you'll need for the next 3 to 5 years
- Financial projections – information like balance sheets

In other words, know everything you can about your business and the industry that you're entering. Your plan needs to show that you're passionate and dedicated, and you actually care about your business.

So, this paragraph amounts to an alert, just like someone told you once to have a resume ready when you applied for your first job. Learn how to properly format a complete and concise business plan.

Conclusions

Whatever your product: wine, steel ball bearings, ceramic tiles or designer clothing, you need to know if your product is of commercial quality. If it is of commercial quality, when you know your production cost, you choose a marketing strategy, such as competing on price quality or value for the money. Being priceworthy in the market place of any industry is key!

Find the proper format for your business plan. The chapters that follow each touch on some aspect of business plan that will help structure your thinking and shape your planning.

3. Licensing and Permits

General business points:

- **Zoning**
- **Licenses**
- **Application fees**
- **Name and Logo**

Renewals

The wine business is an extremely regulated industry. Why? Because wine and other beverage alcohols are a cash cow for the tax man! But how did we get to be such a regulated industry in the first place? For historical context, understand that the United States of America is the only major industrialized nation to ever ban the use and sale of alcohol. Even after the repeal of Prohibition on December 5, 1933, alcohol sales, production, and distribution remained extremely regulated activities.

Zoning

Financially, starting my business at home seemed the best option as my funds were limited. Thankfully, I had about 2,000 square feet of available space in my basement, garage, and storage shed. But I needed a *Conditional Use Permit* from the city to operate in a residential neighborhood.

I set about meeting with neighbors and explaining how the plan would have minimal to no impact on the character of our neighborhood and their quality of life. I was NOT asking for permission to sell retail from the house, just manufacture and sell wholesale. After the crush, all of my activities would take place out of the neighbors' views. The *Conditional Use Permit* application process had an application fee.

In the end, my application was approved.

Licensing

The proper sequence for me to become licensed was: federal government, state government, county government, and finally the city government. Remember that getting the *Conditional Use Permit* preceded applying for any licenses.

Federal license

This was the most extensive application process and included preparation of a plat (floor plan) for the proposed winery space, a wastewater management plan, a list of all my equipment, a national agencies criminal records check, and a $2,000 bond to guarantee payment of wine taxes.

I needed a floor plan drawing, as it relates to the concept of a *bonded* space. A *bonded winery* makes reference to the winery being tax compliant. Here's the deal. Think of a winery as a producer. Then think of the same producer's tasting room as a second but separate business. The tasting room and the winery have a common ownership but the former is a producer and the latter is a retailer. The producer occupies the *bonded* space. The retailer—tasting room—occupies a *tax paid* space. The retailer receives goods from the producer and at the moment of receipt becomes liable for federal and state excise taxes. The plat/floor plan allows the taxing entities—state and feds—to know what taxable goods are in each location, because both locations are under the same roof. It's all about the money

Site inspection visit

After completion of these different parts of the application, an on-site inspection by the compliance section of the Alcohol, Tobacco and Firearms Bureau (ATF)—now known as Alcohol and Tobacco Tax and Trade Bureau (TTB)—verified the information on my application. The same inspection was repeated by the state liquor control authority.

State, county and city licenses

After we obtained the federal permit, the application process—platting, background check, and on-site inspection— were repeated by the State of Idaho.

Once licensed by the state and federal governments, copies of their licenses were required as part of my applications to the county and city. City and county licensings relied on the previous inspections, so their processes were simpler.

Last, but not least, Moscow's Chief of Police had to find me "of good moral character" in order for me to operate a winery.

Business Name and Logo

The federal application required that I have my desired business name and logo. These things are essential marketing tools, but they also serve as identification points used to track my compliance with federal rules.

Choosing name and logo

We chose the name "Camas" because it is a beautiful lily with a special place in the history of the Pacific Northwest. Choosing the Camas Lily also provided us with a logo graphic. When choosing a name and logo you must select a name and logo that are not already in use by another wine-related business. Research for our business name and logo was performed by a consulting intellectual property attorney. I located an artist and sent him pictures of a camas lily as a model for his artwork. The result was a logo that stands out on the shelf.

Logo

The importance of the graphic logo can't be overstated. It is your silent seller. As to what is best for a graphic or logo, there is no right answer. Times change, cultures change, and what is viewed as cool changes. All I can advise is that you take the long view and go with a tasteful logo to represent your brand. My strategy focused on place, and camas flowers were an appealing visual image that related to my physical place, both locally and regionally.

Fictitious business name—Doing Business As

Once the artwork existed and the name was chosen, I needed to register my "fictitious business name," Camas Winery, with the county and city. The name and logo also required registrations with the Idaho Secretary of State and the federal government in order to give me their exclusive use among wineries.

Since the 9-11 attack, banks require a copy of a properly filed fictitious business name before they will accept for deposit or cash checks made out to the business.

Trade names

Trade names are brand names that appear on labels, but they do not pertain to the business entity itself: your sole-proprietorship, partnership or corporation. For example, "Blue Sky Corporation," could adopt and legally sell wine under the label name "Daphne Blossom." In the wine business, you are allowed to possess multiple trade names. A trade name is a product line name, commonly called a brand name. Who does this and why? Gallo for one, bottles wine under multiple trade names.

Suppose you want to create a product at a different price point. Instead of changing the price point you have, adding a second trade name allows you to accomplish this goal without damaging your original market position. The new name(s) is added by the TTB to your basic operating permit.

Application Fees

Each level of government also attached costs to their licensing: $500 for the federal, $300 for the state, $100 for the county, and $200 for the city. These prices have likely changed since 1982. Just be aware that every application comes with a cost.

Required Renewals

The state and federal registrations of names and logos both have expiration dates that you need to track. The length of a registration varies between different states and the federal government. Failing to renew your registration will mean that a key part of your product identity is back up for grabs by a competitor.

Conclusions

Many industries have a necessary sequence to obtaining required licensing or inspections. Food safety, water quality, waste products, and industry approval certifications may apply and may also require a proper sequence. Find out what applies to your intended industry: city business license to approve a facility; product health and safety inspection; industry certification such as "Underwriter's Lab (UL)" on electrical parts, appliances and equipment.

Each step comes with its own learning curve for mastering terminology, formatting of material for application, meeting filing deadlines, and of course, paying the filing fees.

Your business name and logos are types of intellectual property and therefore have economic value. They are your identity and reputation in the mind of the buying public. Choose them carefully and then protect them through registrations with the federal government and separately with each state where you plan to do business. You'll spend money to create your businesss name and logos. You'll spend years creating consumer awareness of your brand and a positive reputation in the market place. Don't waste the time and money you've spent by neglecting to keep ownership of these items.

4. Obtaining Working Capital

General business points:
- **Production Units**
- **Balance**
- **Quitting the day job?**
- **Raising start-up funds**

How much wine could I afford to make in a balanced way according to my available time, space, and money? When I team-taught Entrepreneurship at the University of Idaho, I would ask my class, "What does it cost you to make and sell wine from FREE grapes?" They typically answered, quickly and loudly, "Nothing."

Wrong! Read on...

Thinking in Production Units

One ton of grapes will produce, on average, 150 gallons of finished wine. Depending on the press you are using, your yield could be from 135 to 165 gallons per ton. I'll stick with 150 gallons for my example. Bottled in a traditional twelve-bottle case, this means 750 completed bottles per ton of grapes: about 65 cases, 750 empty bottles, 750 neck foils, 750 corks, and 815 labels per ton of grapes. This is your production unit, and each production unit must be managed as carefully as possible in terms of dealing with costs and available space.

The space needed for 1 production unit (one ton of grapes) is actually double what you might imagine. Here's why. You have 65 cases of empty bottles on 1 pallet waiting to be filled. You also need another empty pallet for those same cases as they are filled.

Bottles

When purchased from a major supplier, bottles are usually sold only in pallet-load units. The same will be true for other glass containers. Hock bottles are palletized in 90-case units, while burgundy or claret shapes are sold in either one-hundred-five-case units or one-hundred-twenty-case units. On rare occasions, bottles can be purchased by the case.

Wine types are usually paired to traditional bottle shapes and sometimes to bottle colors (e.g., Chardonnay, Pinot Gris, and Pinot Noir are bottled in dead-leaf green, burgundy-shaped bottles; Cabernets, Merlot, and Malbec are bottled in green claret-shaped bottles). You may not be making or bottling each variety in every production cycle, so pick bottle shapes and colors that will be usable for multiple wines (i.e., Pinot Gris this year, Chardonnay next year, etc.). This can be an important strategy because storing components between uses risks their getting damaged or dirty. Besides wine bottles there are shelf-life issues with components such as bagged corks or yeast that raise your general operating costs when you have to throw them away.

Corks, neck foils, and labels

Corks, neck foils, and labels are also part of your production unit. Corks are sold in 1,000-count bags, so one production unit of grapes will use 75% of a bag of corks. Of course, once a bag of natural corks is opened, the corks begin to dry out, so be aware of potential shelf-life issues. Neck foils are sold in boxes of 2,500 units per color/size. Labels are usually printed in 1,000 label units, so again you will use less than 100% of these items for one production unit of grapes.

So, the production unit for one ton of grapes includes: neck foils, bottles, corks, and labels, all of which are sold in units whose size exceeds your immediate need for 150 gallons of wine. When calculating your production costs and cash requirements, figure in the cost of all components in their purchase quantities, as opposed to what the same components will cost in a post-bottling "cost of goods sold" or Uniform Capitalization (UCAP) accounting scenario.

Balance

Balance is akin to a three-legged stool involving time, space, and money. Here's how it works. The amount of wine I could make was determined not only by how many tons of grapes I could afford to finish into packaged wine, but also the time it took to create the wine, and the space needed to produce and sell the wine.

If you do not maintain balance in time, space, and money, then your enterprise will fail. It's that simple.

Balance in money

Balance in money is easier to understand once you understand the balance of time and space. There are some problems that money will fix, but sometimes with unintended consequences. You can throw money at a space problem and buy, rent, or build more space. But you would do so at the trade-off of having a larger debt service.

I also had to figure the cost of increasing my equipment from hobby size to small commercial size, as well as the cost of overhead items such as licenses, insurances, and utilities.

Balance was the key and after putting all my research into place, I determined I would need about $18,000 beyond the equipment already on hand to get started. I had researched my equipment needs and balanced these with how much space I had available to make and store the wine and how much time could be found for winemaking. In finding my balance point, the costs of equipment, grapes, and components were now fairly firm numbers. Grapes, as with any other agricultural product, can undergo mild price fluctuations, but their price was foreseeable within a certain price range. That also proved to be true with license fees, insurance coverage, and the creation of labels. The artist's fee, printer's fee, filing fees for copyright, and trademarks were all down on paper.

Balance in space

If I made wine in my home (basement, garage, or yard) to save money, then I could only make as much wine as my available space permits. Production time interacts with spatial needs as I had to have additional space for most—if not all—of my wines to insure the continuity of supply. Because some wines have a long product time, I needed space for barrels from one vintage to be aging while I filled more barrels for the second vintage. In other words, there needed to be a second batch of each wine variety ready to go when I sold the last bottle of the first batch.

Here is an example of balance in space. I hope it helps. I own one 3,000-liter tank (792 gallons). The space footprint of a tank varies according to how it is configured—tall and skinny, short and squat, or in between. My tank was almost exactly a five-foot square; meaning the footprint of my tank was almost exactly twenty-five square feet. The wine from this tank, once bottled, equaled 333 cases. A case equates to twelve bottles each filled with 750 milliliters of wine. I rely on a pallet jack rather than a forklift, and the highest stack of wine I put on a pallet is seven layers, with fifteen cases per layer. For this example, we'll go with Bordeaux bottles, which allows for 105 cases on a pallet.

You may be thinking, "I'll get a fork lift and stack my pallets two high!" That works for empty glass but full glass bottles on two pallets will collapse the bottom layer of bottles under the weight of the stack. A rack system is necessary to safely hold a vertical stack of pallets of full wine bottles. You are trading space for money in this scenario. Even if you rent a forklift instead of buying one, the space you save is greatly diminished by the need to keep larger aisles for the forklift to be able to pivot and operate.

The footprint of the wine bottled from this one tank, results in me now needing the added space for three full pallets and eighteen additional cases, besides the footprint of the tank. As they say on television, "But wait, there's more!" We also need to determine the space for empty glass containers that are waiting to be filled. This adds one more pallet that must be accounted for. So, we're up to four pallets plus the tank; but wait, there's more! Even if you're lucky enough to put the three pallets of bottled wine in a single row, you need to allow aisle space along one side of the pallets for access to the wine so cases can be removed.

How big are pallets? There are two footprint sizes of glass pallets, twenty square feet or twenty-five square feet; we'll use the larger figure for this demonstration. So, the total square footage involved in producing this one tank of wine is: tank at twenty-five square feet, 4 pallets at twenty-five square feet each, for a total of 125 square feet. If aisle space is added, you are up to 145 square feet with one aisle thirty inches wide. This is what balance in space means. The single tank and its contents can't be made salable unless you have more space than that tank alone. Also, remember that your total production of grape wines will likely be divided among several different varieties. So, you need the access to each variety of wine, and this must be configured into your floor space planning.

Balance in time

When I began my business I was willing to work an average of seventy hours a week between my day job and the winery. That meant an average of twenty hours per week for the winery. I could not buy more grapes than I had time or space to process. The actual making of the wine is only a fraction of the time you will spend in your winery. You also need time for bottling, moving the bottled wines to storage, labeling, foiling, repacking, and handling for sale. Selling takes time, whether in making calls on potential customers, delivering, or working in the tasting room.

Quit the day job?

The first significant issue with the balance in time concerned quitting my job to try the business venture full time vs. starting my business as a part-timer while maintaining my existing job and income. This was so important an issue to me that my thinking was quickly resolved.

The dream of a winery was primarily mine so I had no right to put my family at any economic risk. I could make as much wine as time permitted, but only after I had put in my average fifty-hour workweek. Also, since it requires more than a year to turn a ton of red grapes into marketable wine, I would have expenses significantly before some of my wine even came to market. The time element of my balancing act was very uncertain. When would I be able to devote time to necessary winemaking chores?

I met with my boss—not my wife, but the other boss—and made a gentleman's agreement for a week off work at crush time. My part of the agreement was to acknowledge that the demands of my job would always come first.

This was critical because fruit, once picked, has a very limited shelf life before it begins to spoil. I believed I could do all the other winemaking tasks in the evening or on weekends. This would expand my customary fifty-hour workweek to include my winemaking efforts. I was now looking at a workweek of about seventy hours. With the issues of balance addressed, I could move on to the next obstacle: regulation.

Raising Money

The amount of wine I could make was determined by how much money I had or could afford to borrow.

Creative financing

With no track record in the wine industry, going to a bank wasn't a realistic option. I needed to borrow from family or friends. An honest assessment of what I could repay, even if the business failed, was essential to my plan. My proposal included making no payments during the first year, so my loan balance(s) would increase due to interest. Thereafter, I would pay only interest for three years. In the fifth year, I planned to begin repaying the principal and interest amortized over a five-year period. This was necessary because I would have no cash flow for almost a year and no regular revenue stream, assuming I made saleable wine, until I was deep into year two of the winery's life cycle.

Among the investors were my mother, two aunts and uncles, five friends from my local wine tasting group, and one longtime friend, Robert, from California. I provided each with a signed loan agreement, even though many didn't want things reduced to writing. I collected their investment and banked it prior to starting my equipment purchases.

A hard lesson learned

Robert, my best friend, was a successful businessman and he suggested that I simply tell him when his $5,000 was needed. I agreed and, having all my needed funds corralled, I began to order equipment and to contract for grapes. On the day I called Robert for his promised money, I heard, "Stu, the IRS just froze my business accounts over a tax dispute. I'm sorry; I just don't have the money for you."

So, because I treated this friend differently, I had a problem of my own making. I was committed financially to the venture but now lacked the necessary funds. I was the victim of my own unwillingness to enforce business-like procedures with a friend. A criminal defense attorney with whom I had worked once said to me, "What you don't get up front, you don't get!"

Lesson learned, but what to do now? My choices were all undesirable but hard decisions had to be made. I cashed in an insurance policy my parents had taken out for me as a small child. Its surrender value was about $3,000. And I returned to the bank of Uncle Bill, who neither laughed nor refused to loan me another $2,000. I now had the funds I needed.

Conclusions

In any production business, you want to buy your components at wholesale, make your product and then sell it as profitably as you can. Whatever your components may be, they are sold in certain unit sizes: dozens, grosses, thousands or by the pound. You can seldom buy just the number of individual components that you need at one time.

Your unique balance point is a combination of available time, space and money. You can only make as much product as your available space allows, time allows, and money allows. Finding your proper balance point is crucial to buying the right number of components.

Concerning money, keep the following points in mind. Starting out, you might not want to risk an existing income based on your hope/expectation or dream of future income from your start-up. Starting out, you may not be a good risk for a traditional lender.

Create a well-planned borrowing and repayment plan that you can offer to friends and relatives, which benefits everyone. Finally, a promise to pay is just that, a promise. Don't spend money until your financing is actually secured, in-hand or secured by an irrevocable letter of credit.

5. Legal Structure

General business points:
- **Consultants**
- **Corporation**
- **Sole proprietorship**

This I knew; I had no idea about how or why to choose a particular business structure. My previous jobs had been as a school administrator, a cop, and a college teacher. I'd been hired help in several stores, but I'd never owned a business. I'm not as smart as I think I am; just ask my wife!

Consultants

My accountant and my attorney advised me on business documents, zoning issues, and potential liability. My insurance agent became a consultant for insurance and liability issues. Soon, I learned that by merely being honest about what I did not know, I was surrounded by potential sources of help.

Sometimes the answers my consultants provided would conflict. For example, the accountant recommended being a corporation. The attorney suggested a sole proprietorship. What to do? Who to believe? I arranged for them to meet; and for the price of a good lunch, had them explain to each other and to me their recommendations. Each had answered honestly, but without the benefit of the other discipline's perspective on the same question.

Does incorporating give protection?

What I thought I knew—that corporations are shielded from liability—turned out to not always be true. I discovered that if my business was a "mom and pop" enterprise, neither large nor complicated, courts would likely "pierce the corporate shield" if an issue of liability emerged.

My circumstances were not corporate in size, structure, or scope. The best solution to the issue of liability came through interaction with another consultant, my insurance man. It turned out the cheapest and best protection of my assets was a larger liability limit on my several insurance policies—not incorporation.

Sole Proprietorship

Being a sole proprietor means you are the business, and the business is you. Business income flows into your ordinary income, rather than into a separate tax filing as required for a corporation. So, rather than being misled by what I thought, I arrived at the correct answer only after listening to my consultants and combining their advice. We settled on keeping things as simple as possible by creating a sole proprietorship.

Conclusions

Abraham Lincoln was an attorney and once asked a student, "How many legs does a horse have, if we call his tail a leg?"

"Five," said the student.

Lincoln's answer was, "Four legs, because you can call a tail anything you want but it's still not a leg."

Find out what format fits the realities of your business. Incorporation at any level is not a suit of armor that in all cases protects your personal assets. The reality of your size and scope should guide your business format. Check the ever-changing tax code. Remember that incorporation comes with enhanced record-keeping requirements. As your business matures you can always change from one format, say sole proprietorship to a sub-chapter S corporation, when the time is right and your business realities have changed.

6. Equipment

General business points:
- **Adapting equipment**
- **Sourcing equipment: new, used or rental**
- **Shipping**
- **Spare Parts**

Wine production is a costly business with many decisions to be made about equipment. As I learned, there are four aspects to purchasing winemaking equipment: Choosing the right equipment, adapting, sourcing, and shipping. What did I need to augment the small-scale production equipment I already owned? Could I convert some equipment from my wine hobby into my wine business, such as by motorizing my hand-cranked crusher-stemmer? What other essential items did I need to buy because I couldn't adapt, borrow, or rent them? I needed to buy wine specialty items such as a bottleneck foiling machine, a labeling machine, a filter machine, and a bottle-filler. When choosing specialty equipment, I picked items that would meet my needs now and for as long in the future as possible. Finally, I needed to determine the best values among the competing equipment sources.

The Right Sized Equipment

Sometimes it was best to buy slightly larger items than my minimum immediate needs. Depending on the nature of your intended business, this question will manifest in a million different ways. Here is an example of how it came up in mine.

In 1983, if you were starting a small winery, you used a 'basket press'. This is the original style of press: slotted wood staves inside a circle of two round hoops that form the basket. The crushed grapes are poured into the top of the basket and then wooden half-circles are placed on top of the grapes. The mechanical metal press head is ratcheted down, pressing out the juice. The press head descends on a large screw-threaded metal shaft in the center of the basket. The smaller the basket, from one-quarter ton to two tons, the more press loads will be needed to press all your crushed grapes.

The price of the press does not double just because the basket size doubled, so it was cheaper to buy the largest press I could afford. EXCEPT, the threading of the center shaft only goes halfway down. So if I bought a one-ton press because it cost only 50% more than a half-ton press, I couldn't press less than three-quarters of a ton of crushed grapes at one time. Why? Because the press head and wouldn't descend far enough to put sufficient press on the grapes in the bottom of the basket.

Bigger is better—cheaper, but only if it works for both your 'now' and your intended 'then.'

Adapting Equipment

The first aspect of purchasing winemaking equipment is adapting. As an intern in my California neighbors' wineries, I learned to adapt common home and garden items for winery uses. For instance, some types of plastic pipe and vinyl flex tubing from the home improvement store are also fine for winery use. Large plastic drums used for shipping bulk food items adapt well as fermenters. These are some examples of things obtained locally that, while not designed for wine production, worked to save me money while cash was short. I motorized my hand-cranked grape crusher to make it faster and better suited to crushing eight tons of grapes instead of one ton as I did for my hobby.

Sourcing Equipment

If I couldn't adapt or rent a readily available item to my specific needs, buying a piece of specialty equipment was necessary. Once you get a handle on your equipment needs, seek out options in the marketplace. So I had to perform a little more research and locate equipment firms that specialized in small-scale winemaking equipment.

Buying new

Who's got the best price on what you need and how do you locate them? Check your industry trade journals, for this is where suppliers advertise. As you look at options consider the best value in equipment size. Maybe you would do well to buy something slightly larger than immediately needed, as previously explained?

Can you buy used equipment?

I always looked for used equipment. Stainless steel equipment is hard to hurt. With a good cleaning, it is 'forever' stuff. In evaluating the cost-to-benefit ratio between comparable new versus used consider what parts wear out. In refrigeration, cold cases, freezers, motors, and compressors wear out but are easily replaced. In food, machinery, pumps, transport-conveyers, bearings, and motors wear out but are easily replaced. The common denominator is that metal bodies of equipment may show wear/scratches/dents, but are otherwise durable items.

Renting vs. buying equipment

We need the use of some equipment more than we need its ownership. Can you conveniently rent the forklift or scissor lift that you occasionally need? You'll buy the pallet jack that you use on a daily basis, but buying the forklift that gets used once per month may not be a good idea. Not only will you pay to own an item, but you'll have to store and maintain it too. Think about it.

Shipping: the Delivered Price of Equipment

The price of equipment was only half of the price equation. The other half of the equation is any delivery charge. I learned to look not only for the best price, but also for the best delivered price. I found several home winemaking stores in California and Oregon that stocked equipment for my purpose and had great deals on shipping. You can also approach an independent trucker to see if he will be "dead-heading" (coming back from a delivery run with an empty truck). In this way, you can often save a bundle on motor freight shipping.

Spare Parts

When I started in the wine business in Northern Idaho, some of my equipment needs didn't line up with other types of local businesses. Food-grade pump impellers, micro-switches for a semi-automatic corker and many other items were particular to the wine business. The parts and equipment suppliers were all located far out-of-state. For those specialized parts, I always kept a spare part on hand and a file with point of contact and part number for reordering.

Conclusions

When looking to equip your business, think about function first, not ownership. Can I adapt something I already have to perform the function I need? Pretty/shiny/new is nice, but not as nice as saving money. Again, think function first! Remember that the sales price of any item is not the same as the 'delivered price' of the item. Especially when starting out, put your money into things that 'show' in the product, and don't worry about what the production equipment looks like; care about what it does for you.

Keep key spare parts to avoid down time. As plans change and product lines evolve, your equipment needs can change.

7. Marketing Plan

General business points:
- **Matching your market —Zoning**

As previous explained, wines are marketed in four distinct price and quality ranges. There are bulk wines (sometimes called "jug wines"), "the fighting varietal" (low end of varietal wines but better than bulk goods), premium wines, and ultra-premium wines. Based on the advice of my consulting distributor, I sought to place my wines in the middle of the premium price range. He said the proper price point was key; so I opted to vary my profit margin in order to have the wine sold at the desired price. My belief was that if people tried my wines, they would like them. This proved to be true. The trick was to get people to buy that first bottle.

Fitting Product to My Chosen Market Spot

I picked premium wines as my target market. Jug wines and the fighting varietals are high volume—low profit margin wines. Their profitability is based on doing a volume business. To sell lots of wine, you need transportation and distribution networks, both of which I initially lacked. Premium wines have more potential profit per bottle, hence a better fit with my limited production capacity. In order to fit this market, I had to reach targets in the areas of packaging and product quality.

Packaging/Bottles/Labels

Choosing premium meant using appropriate packaging, so 750 ml bottles of the correct shape and color for each different variety of wine. I needed commercial-quality labels with the most advantageous, legal, and correct information on grape varieties and sources. There are lots of details to labeling. The label paper must be right for the adhesive you're using. The paper grain must run in the proper direction. A clear clay coating or varnishing of the label is needed to prevent ink smudging when bottles are boxed or handled. The weight of the paper is also a factor: neither too thin nor too heavy.

Sourcing Grapes

I needed to purchase grapes from reputable growers. While you can make bad wine out of good grapes, you can't make good wine out of bad grapes. I had to produce the wines with quality in mind, such as sufficient aging versus selling wines before they had matured. It was also important to find growers that had as many of my desired grape varieties as possible. A different grower for each different grape would significantly complicate my life.

Producing Quality Wine

How did I become successful at producing and selling wine that was viewed by the public, and my industry, as a quality product?

- I put my available funds into buying quality raw materials. My wine was beautiful; only my equipment was ugly.
- If I made a batch that my consultants didn't like, it was never sold. I fixed it, drank it myself, dumped it, or turned it into another product such as jelly.
- I used consultants and kept an awareness of the limits of my knowledge. When in doubt, which was often, I asked for help.
- I made what the public wanted to buy and not just what I wanted to drink.
- I made sure every promise was honored, every check paid and every deal was a win—win for both parties.

Zoning Limits on How I Sold My Wine

State law, at that time, dictated how I could sell my wine once it had been produced. One of my tradeoffs had been to work from home as a cost-cutting measure. However, the hidden consequence of this decision meant being limited to selling wine to distributors who resold it to stores; If I tried to operate a tasting room out of my home, the local zoning regulations would make me an outlaw. You need to check your local zoning rules for whatever your intended business will be.

Zoning rules and the limits of my *Conditional Use Permit* prevented me from having a tasting room at my home and I could not afford to rent a commercial location for product or tasting. I worked with my distributor and conducted a series of in-store tastings, pouring small samples for shoppers. I provided sample bottles to local restaurants as another means of getting my wines known and to help the distributors help me. As time permitted, I even accompanied distributors in Boise or Spokane on their sales calls. These trips would also include introducing my wines and myself to restaurants and wine shops.

Conclusions

Whatever you're making must be saleable, so picking the correct spot in the competitive market is crucial. All the factors mentioned above: distribution, packaging, marketing opportunities, and production balance issues, need to be considered. As I learned, 'wine is easy to make, it's only hard to sell!' Different price points should be consistent with how you choose to compete; on the basis of price—quality or value. Here again these two points must be balance with appropriate packaging and components.

Sometimes fixed production cost and the limited of a multilevel distribution system will make your 'profit margin' the only variable you can control. Be willing to make less profit on some items instead of risking your distributors and retailers if taking your full profit makes the item non-competitive in the market place.

8. Human Resources Plan

General business points:
- **Using volunteers**
- **Setting up tasks**

So who was going to do all this work? I would handle all the areas of winemaking that required some amount of experience and knowledge, such as monitoring the progress of grape juice to raw wine and then into aged, and finally, saleable bottled wine. However, many hands would be needed during the crushing of the grapes.

Free Labor from Friends: 'Herding Cats'

I found that my friends and neighbors were eager to be involved with winemaking on a short-term basis. I used to say that I used the "Tom Sawyer white-washes a fence" school of human resources.

A truck would show up with tons of grapes, and I'd be there with a rented forklift to unload the bins into my front yard. The next morning, I had neighbors waiting to help. I would assign them to different jobs: loading grapes into buckets from the bins, carrying buckets of fruit to the crusher, moving crushed grapes to the press, pressing, and moving juice. My wife made a giant pot of chili or stew and I had tubs of soda, beer, and wine. My kids helped by playing at working.

There were a few lessons learned from my free labor. Don't be so generous with the free wine that you lose a significant part of your workforce from one day to the next.

Never assume that any task is too simple to need initial supervision. My friend Rocky was placed in charge of my two-ton basket press. Rocky had over-medicated himself with my free oral analgesic—cabernet, I think. He learned that you remove the metal latches (called dogs) holding the two halves of the basket press together only after you've pressed a load of grapes, never before or during pressing, because the partially-pressed grapes in the basket will wind up around your feet. Rocky also learned that if you press too hard too fast, the ten-foot-long spray of juice and crushed grapes has a sobering effect when it hits you in the face and chest. It's a good day when we can learn something.

Conclusions

Labor can be a key component in cutting production costs. With paid employees, labor is more than salary, as it will necessarily include: FICA, unemployment insurance, benefits, training time and perhaps employee fidelity bonding (covers losses due to theft).

Look for and use 'free' help where and when you can. Do you have friends who want to help for the fun or the experience? Are there college interns who want experience in a future career field? Has someone approached you about getting into the same business and wants to 'see what it's like?' Free labor is usually not truly free; be exceptionally nice to your volunteers so they will want to come back. Acknowledge their lack of experience. Break down a volunteer's duties into simple repetitive steps that are easily learned and hard to screw up.

9. The First Few Years

General business points:
- **Raw material acquisition issues**
- **Learning the market**
- **Legal limitations**
- **Continuity of supply**
- **Price point**

The fun begins! It was now time to make some wines! Up to now, I had planned, researched, acquired licenses, raised and spent money, but not made any actual commercial wine. Now, to see if I had made a huge mistake. The first step in this 'moment of truth' was buying grapes.

Sourcing Grapes

Back in 1983, there were few if any grapes grown in the Idaho Panhandle. Some of the very few north Idaho grapes were part of a small experimental planting program done by the University of Idaho in the early 1970s. I tracked one such experimental plot to a Lewiston cherry orchardist and worked out a trade—his grapes for my pruning his neglected vineyard. This small vineyard, planted to test different varieties, had too few vines of any one type to label as a varietal wine. The federal government requires a wine to be seventy-five percent of one particular grape for varietal labeling. So, I opted to blend all these grapes into one blush-style wine.

Commercial growers

The nearest commercial source of grapes was the Columbia Valley of Washington State. Being a wine drinker and belonging to a local wine tasting club, I had some general knowledge of Columbia Valley growers. I approached the largest grower, whose fruit was well known and highly regarded, and was able to contract for premium grapes in multi-ton quantities. I chose grape varieties that I was familiar with—Chardonnay and

31

Cabernet Sauvignon. Two of my first three wines would be dry, while the blush-style would be fruity and slightly sweet.

Not haggling over grape prices

Price was not a significant factor in my choice of grower or grape varieties. I did not haggle over the price with the grower because he had no trouble selling his grapes and I, as an unknown, might be a one-time customer. In other words, I needed him more than he needed me. Having grown grapes and made wine as a hobbyist, I knew that the quality of finished wine can never exceed the quality of the grapes used. Or to put it another way, you can't make chicken salad out of chicken shit.

Learning the Market and Adjusting Grape Varieties

I believed my wine was good, based on what a growing number of distributors were telling me; their customers found my wines to be a good value. In my mind, I saw myself as the "village winemaker." I knew what was selling but I had no specific idea of who was buying my wine. Men or women? Which age groups or income groups? Students or parents? What kinds of wine did people in Moscow drink? The problem of not knowing my customer base was readily solvable. I did my due diligence by asking distributors, restaurants, and stores; who were the folks that were actually buying?

As I learned more about my customers' preferences I switched from two-thirds dry wines to one-third dry and two-thirds sweet (the percentage of sweetness among my offering in later years ranged from two percent to ten percent residual sugars). Listening to your customers and learning what they want is the key. If we persist in making what we ourselves like, that is a hobby. If we can learn to make what the customer wants, that is a business.

Another Legal Limit on Sales

In 1983 the State of Idaho did not allow wine producers to sell directly to retail stores or restaurants, meaning a distributor was essential. At that time there were only three distributorships in Moscow. The distributor who had helped as my consultant agreed to sell my wines to his local accounts. This distributor also had a storage warehouse in Boise, so he could offer my wine to store and restaurant accounts there. A second local distributor agreed to sell my wine in a different area. By 1985, I had grown successful enough to approach distributors in Coeur d'Alene, Idaho, and in Spokane and Pullman, Washington.

Victim of My Own Success: Selling Out too Quickly

Of my three initial wines, the first release came in May 1984, and the 160 cases of blush-style wine sold out in two months. Wow, how could I not be a success after a start like that? However, the quick sale of my blush wine created a new problem: supplying the market. I had nothing else ready to sell. I feared that I would lose my newfound places on shelves. I had to come up with a new wine, and fast. Retail outlets want to develop a clientele for a particular wine and be assured their customers will not be disappointed by their favorite wine being out of stock.

A stop-gap solution

The orchardist who'd supplied grapes for my blush wine had a batch of cherries available. These cherries could not be sold as table-fruit, either because of their size or cosmetic blemishes, so I used them to develop a red grape and cherry combination. This unusual mix, which required special government approval to make, allowed me to take part of my bulk Cabernet Sauvignon that was not yet aged enough to be saleable and bring it to market early. The cherry-grape combination tasted better chilled than most red grape wine. It sold at a lower price point than cabernet. The cherry grower got a return on a portion of his crop that in prior years he had merely discarded. Everybody wins!

(Back to) Market research

My research and experience revealed that many Midwesterners and novice wine drinkers prefer their red wines to be lightly sweet and served chilled. My new cherry-grape wine fit this profile. Additionally, my local distributor's supervisor mentioned he would love to include in his listings a red wine that retailed for $5 per bottle. Most well-known red grape varieties, such as Merlot or Cabernet Sauvignon, could not be produced and retailed at $5 by wineries of my size. However, my blending of grape and cherry wines could meet that price range, and it would also cover the gap in availability of product until my first dry wines were sufficiently aged. My crisis became a win for the cherry grower, winemaker, distributor, and customer! I now had a fourth wine that bridged the gap between the release of my blush and the release of my two dry varietals.

A niche product was born by accident rather than design, and this serendipity launched the most profitable segment of my business. Continuing to make uncommon wines helped me survive the onslaught of inexpensive Australian and Chilean wines that began to glut the market.

Two new wines were added in 1984, and a third in 1985, bringing my product line to seven wines with a total production of 2,500 gallons or a little more than 1,000 cases. All profits were poured back into the business in the form of better equipment, increased capacity and enlarged promotional efforts. Choosing to keep my day job allowed my business profits to help grow the business.

Price Worthiness: Why It's Critical

Price competitiveness was crucial for the distributor because of their limited shelf-space allocation. Chain stores allot linear shelf space to each distributor and largely allow the distributor to choose which wines to stock in each store.

What the big retailer wants from the supplier

The store's concerns are two-fold; whatever is on their shelf must produce a certain level of profit and must have a high turnover rate. The store's profit/pricing system operates on the dual principals of profit and turnover; make a small profit, over and over.

For example, a gallon of milk only has a two percent (or less) profit margin, but no individual gallon is in the store for more than a few days, so the store makes a two percent profit on multiple sales within a week's time from the same bit of shelf space. New, unusual, or specialty items that may have a slow turnover rate are less likely to get into the store because of limited shelf space. Some producers forget about the turn as a key to their retailer's thinking. By setting their profit margin too high, the net result is they shoot themselves in the foot! Ouch!

Who gets the shelf space?

Large distributors receive pressure from major national wine brands to move quotas of their wine, or lose access to the brand. Suppose the distributor has our micro-sized winery and a big national brand as clients. The distributor will have on their shelves every item in the national brand's inventory—all displayed at the best spots (eye level) —and then will fill any leftover spaces in the less desirable spots with my brand. This is because the distributor needs the national brand and does not need me. In fact, until 1987, the distributor didn't need me at all. I, on the other hand, needed him because I had no tasting room and was legally unable to sell directly to stores or restaurants.

Small retailers

The best place for my small premium brand was in specialty shops. Specialty shops are usually owner operated, so buying decisions are made in-house and not at a corporate headquarters. Specialty shops, wine shops, gourmet food shops, and wine bars want items that are not in every grocery store. Finally, specialty shops take the time to know their products and their customers so they can better 'hand-sell' items. Hand selling is when the retailer can provide recommendations and product information to customers about your special products.

Conclusions

Learn if your product requires any special approvals to be sold in a particular geographic market. Do you need label approval, pasteurization of food items, or lab certification of purity, ingredient, or nutritional content?

Big chain stores such as grocery, hardware, and clothing want continuity of supply. They may buy only once if your product doesn't sell, but they still want to know that more is available if it does sell. All stores, and especially chain stores, sell for less per unit mark-up but make their money on "the turn;" how many times they can sell the same item from the same shelf space. If your product doesn't sell fast enough to meet their expectations, bad things happen. The retailer is unhappy with the distributor and the distributor is then unhappy with you; don't price yourself out of the market. Pick your best price point to be competitive in the market place. Consider if your product/price point is best suited for small versus large retailers

Sometimes market research is done before acting. Sometimes you need to do more research because of unforeseen circumstance. In either case, be creative, listen to your consultants and strive to create long-term win-win situations for yourself as well as your suppliers and retailers. Knowing the demographic of your customer base and their ability to pay is essential for any product.

10. Bit on the Ass by Reality

General business point:
- **Overhead**
- **Changing the business model**
- **Changing location**

As you'll see, I didn't learn fast, but I did learn good. When my success was discovered to be something of an illusion or at best an ego trip rather than a business, I didn't give up. More market research and two years of hunting and planning finally led me to a profitable long-term solution.

Checking the Pulse of Your Business

In the spring of 1987, I had an epiphany about where I was in terms of the success or progress of the winery. At of the end of the 1986 sales year, 800 cases of wine had been sold from the 1,000 cases produced. This meant I'd sold virtually the entire annual product that was ready for sale. Remember, some products require different lengths of time to mature, so not all become saleable at the same time. The bad news was that on these 800 cases, my wife/bookkeeper determined that I had made a total profit of about $1,200, or $1.50 per case. I believed that I would make $1 per bottle for a minimum of $12 per case, or almost $9,600 total. How could I have been so wrong? How could I have been working so hard for so little? How could I have blown so much sunshine up my own ass?

True Costs in Calculating Overhead

It turned out that my single-minded dedication to producing quality wine was almost my downfall. I had not realized, nor been willing to hear, that my true production costs should have included:

- cost of all my promotional expenses for advertising;

- cost of providing free samples;
- cost of travel to pours (free wine poured at wine-related events as a marketing tool); and
- cost of delivering to distributors.
- I should have also been including the apportioned costs of my home production space, water, and utilities.

All of these expenses, which were real but not previously factored into my thinking, had to come out of my thirty percent of the wines' profit that I received.

In truth, I was succeeding at being a producer and yet failing at being a businessman. Having kept a day job allowed me room for mistakes and to recover rather than fail. I was sadder but wiser. What I had learned in my first four years meant finding a new strategy if I wanted to become a financial success.

Changing/Adapting My Business Model

As a result of my epiphany, I started paying more attention to details regarding overhead expenses and began being more honest with myself as a businessman. Secondly, to maintain the necessary balance of time, space and money I needed to make the same amount of wine but sell it at a higher profit level. *Remember: It is not how much money you take in, but how much money you keep!* In 1986, the only option for making more money was to capture more of the profit on each case of wine sold. This meant I needed to open a tasting room.

Changing Location

Retail space could be at a different location from my product space or share one location. To maintain my balance in time, space and money, I wanted one location.

Assessing needs

Looking at possible locations meant dealing with zoning issues or possibly another *Conditional Use Permit* application. The new site would need customer parking. How did any storefront look? Was the interior and exterior lighting satisfactory? Were there improvements needed to make the space usable as a tasting room? Did the potential site already have counters or display spaces? These questions dealt with the needed retail space.

I also had my production space needs to consider. Did the site have floor drains and was it wired properly (for 110v, 220v and three phase equipment)? Was there room to store all the equipment plus make and store all the wine? Did the site have access for delivery trucks bringing pallets of bottles or taking out pallets of wine? Would it allow for expansion when I retired from my day job?

Site selection

When I started looking for a retail location that combined production and tasting room facilities, my mental image was of a bucolic, rural location. I had in my mind the wineries I'd been around, patronized, and known as neighbors.

I looked at five sites during a two-year period, four of which were outside of town. One local farm that was available had parking, highway access, production and retail space, power and water. When this 'hot prospect' came around, I checked with the country on zoning and with the state health district on water quality. I learned that if I was on my own well, the water would require monthly lab analysis for safety and purity, if it was being used in any aspect of food/wine product, including rinsing equipment. A monthly water source contamination test was at my own expense. The well-head had to be a certain minimum height above ground level, which it was not. There were no similar requirements if I was on city water and sewer. I chose instead to keep on looking for a better location without the water hassles.

The hassles related to domestic water and wastewater management caused me to settle on finding a spot in Moscow. I would trade off some production conveniences and parking for no water problems. Locating my tasting room in town also meant increased foot traffic and higher public awareness. Most available spaces downtown came with prohibitive rents so I continued to search until I found a spot that allowed me to strike a balance in time, space, and money.

Finding a diamond in the rough

I looked at a building that once housed both a meat processing plant and retail butcher shop. It had been vacant for more than two years, and the building was for sale. The previous owner had made extensive improvements and turned a children's clothing store into a food production and retail space. These features actually hurt the resale value of the property for most potential buyers, but they were all positive items for my plans. The space needed work, especially the second floor, which had four ancient low-rent apartment units that had fallen into disrepair. The building's zoning allowed and encouraged a mixed-use business that both manufactured and retailed a product. The retail shop space even came with a large counter. The building was a diamond in the rough, but it was the perfect diamond for the unique needs of my winery.

The building's sale price was $10 per square foot, which translated to an $85,000 purchase price. We could either sell our home and move into the upstairs of the building, or raise our debt load by adding the equivalent of a second house payment. Buying the building and renovating the upstairs could be covered by the profit from selling our home. We chose to sell our home and avoid a second mortgage payment.

Moving licenses/permits when moving locations

In anticipation of opening the tasting room in our new building, I needed to arrange a seamless transfer of my several licenses from our home to the new building. Licenses for alcohol at all the governmental levels allow you to operate only at a specific location. Simply by informing the city, county, state and feds that I would be moving on a specific date allowed me to move my operation without any time gaps or delays. After transferring all my licenses and permits to the new location, and, for the federal authorities, we platted my space and scheduling and completing a site inspection. We moved into the commercial building and opened the tasting room in August 1989.

Overhead adjustments based on my new location

I had corrected the flaw of not seeing or acknowledging the true extent of overhead costs. Starting with the opening of our tasting room in August of 1989, I began to pay the true overhead costs. The winery now paid a percentage of the mortgage on the building and assigned percentage shares of the building's property tax, general liability insurance and fire insurances.

The business continued to pay the full cost of its product liability insurance and newly added liquor legal insurance. Liquor legal is a special type of liability insurance that is necessary when you are pouring alcoholic beverages for tasting purposes or for sale by either the glass or bottle. Liquor legal insurance covers situations that general liability insurance does not cover, such as when an over-served customer falls down the stairs in the wine bar or an on-premises altercation occurs between two customers.

Other necessary adjustments

Our family of four, plus a cat and a dog, lived in one of the four upstairs apartments while the other three units were being transformed into our new home. If you ever want a test for your marriage, living in a one-bedroom apartment with a family of four and two pets is a good one. Lying there at night, my sleep interrupted by dog farts and the longhaired feline sleeping between my bride and me, I questioned, "Why Lord?" Nietzsche is credited with saying "What doesn't kill us makes us stronger!" I wonder what kind of dog he had?

Conclusions

Be honest with yourself about the success and profitability of your enterprise. What feels good to our ego may not be good for the rational, goal directed part of our brain. If something is out of balance, acknowledge it and fix it. Never hang up your learning alongside the licenses on the wall.

Keep abreast of legal changes. Idaho changed its liquor laws to allow me to sell direct to wholesale customers. This change, along with the market's acceptance of my product, enabled me to consider and then adopt a new business model; selling from a combination tasting room/production facility. When looking at potential locations, go as slowly as necessary and keep looking until the right place comes along. Pick a location that fits your sales model and can be adapted to meet your production space needs. Check if your new location requires permission from your city or county. Adjust your overhead to include the realities of your new location.

11. Setting up a Retail Sales Shop

General business points:
- **Retail requirements**
- **New product opportunities**

The options and physical limitations for your fledgling business will be unique. You might need access to a rail spur or an airport for shipping finished product. The same issues could apply for receipt of raw materials. Do you need high foot traffic because you are selling retail? How about a loading dock to ship or receive from motor freight carriers? Customer parking? Access to particular infrastructure features such as natural gas or municipal water? Think carefully, research even more carefully because the consequence of leasing or buying what turns out to be the wrong location can be fatal to a business.

Retail Requirements

Each business is different. I've already mentioned a few key points to keep in mind when choosing a location. The following list of suggestions and comments should also be weighed against the particulars of your situation.

Check your local fire codes for occupancy, fire extinguisher, fire-door, and door-clearance requirements.

Remember the Americans with Disabilities Act (ADA) requirements for door sizes, handicapped-accessible restrooms, and handicapped-accessible seating options. If you offer seating for by-the-glass service, you must have an ADA-compliant service area. The ADA-compliant area must be a part of your larger service area, not hidden away in a back room. Be warned, there are disabled folks who have sued wineries for not being ADA compliant.

Maximize the size of counter space for tasting and place a variety of wines in nearby floor displays. Floor displays with shelf-talker information cards describing and pricing each wine allow guests to browse while waiting to taste or while deciding what to taste. Arrange your floor displays to make it difficult for wine to walk out without being purchased. Have your most valuable goods on display in your best-supervised spots.

Remember that wine is adversely affected by heat, sunlight, and vibration. Arrange your tasting room so the hot afternoon sun will not fall on wine bottles. You may not be able to avoid this problem completely, but you can certainly reduce the problem through careful arrangement of displays. Window shades and window trimmings are a great way to minimize sun-related problems.

Card for age all your guests before serving or selling them beer or wine. Train your staff to card without exception. Allowing staff to decide whom they will or won't card is a dangerous practice. While carding the sixty year old is unnecessary, the twenty-five-year-old woman looks a lot like the twenty-year-old girl who is not allowed to drink. Be safe. Failure to card will result in large fines and potential loss of your state licenses. You can be out of business very quickly. You personally can always waive carding on customers you know or whom you feel are obviously over twenty-one.

There were two alcohol sting problems at my winery in twenty-eight years. In both instances, the involved staff person had been trained to card customers and, in fact, did card the undercover liquor control agent on a busy day. In both instances, the clerk looked at the license and made the mental error of miscalculating age. Even trained staff can make mistakes, but both problems occurred when the boss was not on the sales floor.

If you use display bottles of wine, make a visible mark on the bottle so a display bottle will not accidentally be sold as new merchandise. Display bottles can be of unknown quality or vintage and their sale is very risky.

Have a lockable cash register that is simple to use but not so simple that its daily and monthly readings don't tell you, by category, what you are selling. After closing for the night, keep the register drawer open with the silver coins still inside. The cost of repairing or replacing a cash register that burglars force open is more than the value of a few lost coins.

New Opportunities

Packaging sizes

In addition to the traditional 750 ml bottle, I began putting my wines in a smaller 375 ml bottle. These were a good fit for single people, picnics, gift baskets, and sampler selections. I added sweet white and sweet red dessert wines. The extra sizes and wine types increased my shop's selection and appealed to customers' needs.

Accessories

We also added wine accessories such as corkscrews, wine glasses, and gift bags. The mark-up on these products was good. Offering a wide selection of wine-related products made us a one-stop source for all things wine.

Repurposing a product

The new retail space even provided us with a means to retool slow-moving products into moneymakers. We'd notice that wine-based food items sold well in our tasting room. When a new variety of wine, a wonderful dry rosé, did not sell quickly enough, it was turned into wine jelly and wine vinegar. A probable loss was turned into a profit.

Wine Flights

Consider a wine flight program in which you sell several small glasses of different wines for a set price. For the customer, this program is a bridge between the one-ounce tasting option and the by-the-glass, six-ounce serving. To implement this program, you will need serving trays and smaller glasses. I used three-ounce dessert wine glasses. Print some simple coaster sheets for your serving trays so you can identify for the customers which wine is which.

Conclusions

Think about how everything you make must be sold, perhaps multiple times. Your raw materials have to go in and out, so think about what location serves these twin purposes best.

The biggest issue is, are you principally selling retail? If so, foot traffic and customer parking become crucial. If you are principally manufacturing or selling wholesale then your key issues will be more along the lines of shipping and receiving. Your showroom will utilize floor space and counter space differently according to your business model.

Finally, when choosing a location, check with the regulatory agencies that will be involved. Just like my lucky discovery of the well-water issues, really try to learn as you look.

12.   Competing With the Big Guys

General business points:
- **Marketing strategies**
- **Contract work**
- **Wholesale channels**
- **Research strategies**
- **Adding products**

I've explained how I chose my price point, premium wines, because that spot competes on value, as opposed to being a volume-based business. Because I couldn't afford the time or money to produce large amounts of wine, niche opportunities were viable and valuable options. This was thinking outside the box!

With three nearby universities who each had ROTC programs, one law school and multiple Greek living groups, custom labels with organization logos was an option. Besides the three universities, there was also a private Christian college. Colleges mean graduations, weddings, and military commissioning; the customer base keeps turning over as new students arrive every year.

Contract product work was another option because each batch was presold. Finally, by seeing what worked for other wineries, I carefully researched a major change to my marketing strategy and successfully implemented the change.

Custom Labels, Trademarks and Parody

The best way to compete with the big guys is to make good wine at a good price and earn a reputation for customer service! One of the more successful service-based additions to my product line was custom messaging options for wine bottle labels. After acquiring government approval, I began to laser print personalized messages on wine labels—for example, labels can be printed with messages such as "Happy Anniversary,"

"Merry Christmas from John and Linda,, and "From the private cellar of John Smith," Priced reasonably, it was an attractive enhancement for the customer. With the success of these labels, I sought ways to increase that section of my product line. Next came labels with a local Christian College logo and a special University of Idaho law school label featuring the scales of justice. I even expanded into a series with the emblems of the four branches of our military and featuring a gold bar, the emblem of rank for newly commissioned lieutenants and naval ensigns. All of these labeling options made my product special for the customer.

Using parody to avoid a trademark problem

I was careful to avoid any images previously trademarked by the university. To have a wine label that had some connection to the universities but did not have trademark problems, I consulted an intellectual property attorney. I designed a label that was a parody and created a new wine to go with the label. The label featured the Mona Lisa with a sheep's face replacing Mona's. The wine was called Ewe Eye White, and the graphic image was a parody of the Mona Lisa. Thanks to a case brought against Larry Flint, the U.S. Supreme Court has held parody to be a protected class of speech. Any similarity between the spoken name of this wine, Ewe Eye, and the name of our state university was, of course, purely coincidental. Ewe Eye White might have been clever anywhere, but especially in Moscow, Idaho, home of the University of Idaho.

Producing Wine on a Contract Basis

A year after moving downtown, I was asked to make honey wine (mead) on a contract basis. This offer developed into another successful line. Making wine on a contract basis had the advantage of allowing me to expand my product line. What was especially attractive was the concept of pre-sold inventory. Another advantage was the timing of creating honey wine. Before each season's grapes were ripe, my wine producing equipment sat idle. Honey wine could be made during this time, which resulted in a higher profit margin because I was making further use of my production equipment. As an added bonus, making wine on a year-round basis allowed me to assign percentages of my overhead to many more production units.

What went wrong

Seven years passed and the viability of the contract production program began to change, not because of its failure but rather stemming from its success. I discovered that the other party was exploring his options. He wanted to go with an out-of-state producer that would make the product for less money. Things fell apart; lawyers for both sides got involved and off to court we went. Issues concerned production formulas and registration of trade names—items attorneys refer to as intellectual property, a concept that was unknown to me until it "bit" me. The lesson for me was simple—what is not an issue in good times can become an issue, so clarify in writing to the maximum degree possible.

Two years later, the matter was settled out of court after turning to professional mediation services. Both parties perceived they got what they needed, but at mutual expense. How did this happen and what did I learn from this expensive, disruptive, and upsetting experience? Many of the problems had their roots in the fact that our original agreements, made in 1990, were either handshake deals or informally written agreements. Our best efforts at convivial agreements failed to clarify the future complexity of our relationship. The moral of the story is to plan for the worst while hoping for the best.

Sparkling Wine and Tax Rates

In 1996, with the help of my consultant and mentor, I taught myself to produce hand-made sparkling wines. Sparkling wine can only legally be called Champagne if made in the Champagne region of France. The business of sparkling winemaking demands both enhanced winemaking skills and a masochistic streak.

My entry into this world came in response to consumer demand. If a customer asked for a particular wine that I did not make, such as a Zinfandel, I could suggest a substitute such as Merlot. But there was no substitute for sparkling wine. People might change grape varieties, but if they wanted bubbles, then bubbles there had to be!

At that time, the federal excise tax on sparkling wine was $3.40 per gallon, or $0.68 per bottle, as opposed to $0.03 per bottle for still-wines from small producers! These numbers become important in the section on mark-up and pricing strategies, where I use the still-wine tax rate that the distributor pays. The extra $0.65 of federal tax on sparkling wine increases the retail price of each bottle by $1.10.

Advantages to adding this product

I was operating surrounded by colleges: weddings, graduations, and commissionings are all big events often celebrated with champagne. Being able to provide champagne to a celebration also gave me a leg-up on selling all the wine needed for rehearsal dinners or other celebrations. Add to this my ability to offer custom labels for everything that memorialized weddings, commissionings, and graduations: dates, degree awarded, service branches or names of the bride and groom.

Researching a Marketing Strategy Change

Later that same year (1996), the next big change in marketing arrived. Observing other wineries and the practices that worked for them drove this change.

While in Missouri, I spent a weekend touring local wine country. Absolutely every winery I visited either had a restaurant or wine garden on premises where their wines were served to the public. This idea of selling wine not only by the bottle but also by the glass was obvious and powerful. For example, the profit on one case of Riesling wine could jump from $18 per case on a distributor sale, to $24 per case on a direct sale to a store, to $48 selling the same case directly to a retail customer. If I sold the same case of wine at $5.00 per glass in my store, the profit on the same volume became $168! While I could not make more wine without expanding my production facility, I could easily make more money on my wine by capturing more of the end profit.

Research before proceeding

The cost of adding an on-site consumption area to my tasting room included extra license fees, construction costs, and furnishings. Local restaurants were surveyed to gauge the potential business volume of serving by the glass. With an estimate of potential sales volume and enhanced profitability, it appeared that the $26,000 required for adding a wine bar to my tasting room area would be recouped in a reasonable amount of time.

If you have a wine bar or by-the-glass area, have it separate from, but within sight of, your tasting counter. Not only do you want tasters to see that they have a by-the-glass option, but you also want the ability to move tasters to the drinking area to avoid a line at the tasting counter.

Cost-to-benefit ratio

Will the space you are acquiring or creating generate enough income to cover the added debt service and still increase your profitability? If the extra space does not support itself in terms of income generated within a maximum of five years, then ask yourself, "Should I do this?" This is called "The rule of five," a generally accepted business yardstick for evaluating purchase or expenditure options. This rule is valid for spending your own money. On borrowed money, the income needed to justify the expense is increased by the cost of debt service. Remember the concept of production units. It's never enough to have the money to build something if you don't also have money for furnishings, fixtures, and staffing.

As you consider some type of expansion, remember that equipment or furnishings can be acquired slowly. Maybe you can find a deal on something, then purchase and store it until needed. I did this with furniture for my wine bar. Or maybe you can finish a desired expansion with something less than your ideal furnishings or equipment. Remember that you can sometimes manipulate the time factor to stretch your money.

Taking free knowledge where you find it

During the research process for this expansion, a new consultant emerged from an unexpected source. The most valuable single design suggestion for my new consumption area came to me from a local building inspector. He explained how fire and occupancy codes were more generous with certain configurations of space than with others. By listening to an expert and keeping in mind what I did not know, I got valuable guidance about how to best fit my needs within the confines of the regulations.

My tip for you, dear reader, is not to wait until you've invested in plans and obtained permits to meet with the local inspectors. Ask for informal meetings or site visits from the building department before you spend money with architects, engineers or draftsmen.

Our new wine bar opened in late 1997. Business started more slowly than I anticipated but it soon became a healthy and growing source of revenue. With the new wine bar in place, I kept listening, learning, and tweaking my in-store marketing program. I chose not to operate the wine bar after tasting room hours based on the balance of trading potential wine bar revenue with simplicity and fewer demands on my time. Evening hours would also require either paying overtime or creating a second shift of employees. Finding and retaining reliable employees was always a problem.

The Next Controlled Marketing Change: Adding Beer

Just as a customer could not be finessed from sparkling wine into still wine, a beer aficionado was rarely persuaded into drinking wine. If one member of a group wanted beer and I could not provide it, the entire group was likely to go elsewhere. No problem. A beer license and display cooler were added. While beer was not part of my original wine bar plan, a potential problem became an asset when I developed a wide selection of premium imported beers. Promoting our large beer selection was actually a draw for new customers, who in turn might buy wine gifts or even discover my wine for themselves. Being sensitive to customers' needs will always serve to turn problems into assets. By the time I sold the business in 2011, beer sales represented about 17% of my business.

Conclusions

Twice now I had made the mistake of not doing things in a business-like manner when dealing with friends. Please learn from my mistakes and remember, as a good German friend told me, "Business is business and schnapps is schnapps." Go overboard on clarity. As my first Witness Protection Case (WITSC) supervisee told me, "Stu, faded ink on the most yellowed paper is brighter than the clearest memory."

Steal ideas from your competitors, just not intellectual property. See if what works for them will also work for you. Can you make your product more about the customer through some form of customization? It's all about them, so let them pick colors, packaging, and label designs, as far as practical in your industry.

Remember "The Rule of Five" when considering the value of a potential investment, especially if the change is a "lease holder improvement" that will remain with the rented premises and not follow you to a new location nor become a saleable asset. Finally, does one change in your operation open the door or suggest another possible change, such as adding a wine bar created an option for me to sell beer.

13. Using Before Tax Dollars, Not After Tax Dollars

General business points:

- **Tax avoidance strategy**

Good, bad, or indifferent, I have had a variety of employment experiences, including seven years of lecturing in the College of Business at the University of Idaho. In classes on entrepreneurship and business strategies, I introduced students to the concept of before tax dollars, which deals with maximizing legitimate business deductions.

Here's the deal. Some business expenses are what I call dual use expenses, or expenses that are a legitimate business deduction but also provide a personal benefit to you. Let's suppose you are attending a wine seminar or equipment trade show in the same town where you are visiting relatives or taking a vacation. Because you are attending a genuine business function, a large percentage of your out-of-pocket costs may be dual use expenses. These include travel to the event site, lodging, and some of your meals. What would NOT be deductible, for example, would be the dinner with friends that occurs a full day after your event ended. I am not an accountant nor a tax attorney. Please consult competent professionals about what is allowable for your own business situation.

Paying for dual use expenses from your business checking account increases the buying power of every dollar due to your ability to deduct business expenses from your tax returns. If you paid for those same expenses with after-tax dollars (i.e. dollars left in your account after you have already paid your taxes to the government), your buying power would be reduced by the amount of your tax rate. So with a nominal twenty-five percent tax rate—your winery's tax rate can vary based on being a corporation or a sole proprietorship—you're looking at a twenty-five percent increase in actual buying power when paying your business expenses with pre-tax dollars. Remember though, that even with the advice of your accountant and the maximizing of your legitimate deductions, you still must have the money to pay the bill.

To Cheat the Taxman or Not?

There are lots of opportunities to hide income when you are self-employed, but there are risks. The obvious risk is getting caught, which is a federal felony. The other, less visible but more important, reason not to hid income is the need to show an income trail when you are selling the business. Unless you can prove an income stream sufficient for a buyer to both repay a loan and make profit, bank financing will not be available.

Conclusions

In the long run, it is not good business to cheat the taxman. Why? Obviously the risk, but more importantly, when you go to sell your business you need to show a steady pattern of earnings. Your prospective buyer must convince a bank that there is sufficient income to service their loan and support the cash flow: overhead—salaries—and raw materials purchases. Finally, a tip from a one-time fed. Filing a false tax return is a felony but failing to file a tax return is a misdemeanor. Just saying.

14.   Labels and Related Ideas

General business points:
- **Regulations**
- **Strategies for saving money**
- **Label design issues**
- **The hidden, interactive complexity of packaging**

Packaging turns out to be way more complicated that it first appears. Remember that I'm writing about what I learned, based on the mistakes that I survived. I survived buying the wrong-for-me label machine and finally sold it to a friend, losing $10,000 by overestimating my own mechanical aptitude. Remember, I never said I learn fast, but I do learn good.

Just a teaser here, with more to follow. In paper labels on glass containers, the grain of the paper must be correct for the label to apply flat. The adhesive on your label will be different if the containers might get wet, like a wine bottle in an ice bucket. The paper label needs a lacquered topcoat to prevent smudging and minimize scuffing when labeled bottles are put into a cardboard case. The weight of the paper must be correct for labels.

Fear and dread not; label pros know these things, but the local guy who prints your business cards probably will not.

Regulatory Issues

Wine labels must be approved by the TTB before you can use them on your product. Similarly, there are labeling requirements for prepared food products. Finally, after 9/11, there were requirements for wine and food producers to keep documentation on the sources of their raw materials. Whatever your business, there may be labeling rules, so check them out.

Sometimes the TTB will do a site visit and a 100% review of your records. They will check if your labels are approved and compliant. You must, for example, use certain font sizes. You must show the alcohol content of the wine and indicate if it contains sulfites. The listed alcohol content must be correct within certain tolerances. Alternatively, you can use the term "table wine" if your product falls within certain pre-set limits. There are rules about the use of varietal grape names and appellations of origins.

I found it priceworthy to use a label approval service to proof my labels before their submission. Label approval services are fee-for-service, so there is a nominal cost for you. I paid $15 per label. After your label is approved, you must keep all your approved label forms on file at the winery.

With the advent of on-line submission for TTB label approval, you may want to perform your own label submissions rather than using a label approval service. However, electronic approval comes with a caveat. When you read the TTB online form, you will see that they can approve your sample label even if the sample is not fully compliant with their rules. The TTB online approval process grants approval to print labels provided the actual printed labels are fully compliant with all type size and typeface requirements. Check TTB Form 5100.31 at Section II, CONDITIONS OF THIS CERTIFICATE (C).

Allowable minor label changes

On the reverse side of Form 5100.31 are listed twenty-four common label changes. The form lists which of these changes require new label approval and which do not. For example, any change to the stated alcohol by volume percent content requires a new label approval. However, deleting any language that appears before "bottled by"—such as produced by, hand-crafted, made by, blended, cellared, vinted, or prepared (27 Code of Federal Regulations, 4.35a(III)(IV)(V))—can be done without getting new approval. Using labels with only "bottled by" will save having two sets of labels for the same type of wine if you sometimes sell wine that you have obtained in bulk wine transfer from another bonded producer. If your plan is to make all of your own wine—and thus be able to use the magic words "produced by" or "made by"—then as long as you have produced seventy-five percent or more of the wine that's in the bottle, you are good to go.

Font size

Wine labels required certain minimum font sizes on the legally required information and not just one font size for everything. The font size also could change according to the packaging size.

Non-Standard: Formula Wines

If you plan to combine two categories of wine into a single variety, (fruit and grape, honey and grape or fruit) you must also have approved copies of any formulas that you are using. The formula tells what is to be in the finished wine by percentage of volume and the processes you used in the wine's production. Formula approval is required before you produce any wine that combines any two categories of wines as defined in 27 Code of Federal Regulations (CFR) Part 1. Once your Formula is approved, you must show the approved formula number on your label approval application.

Tips To Save Time, Money and Headaches

Check the rules

See if you need a new label approval when you are making a small change, such as vintage date, on an already approved label.

Labels without a vintage date

These never become obsolete unless you change the state from which you source your fruit.

I used custom labels for special events and for my house brands. Why would these labels be wasted? The cheapest overall way to limit label costs is to purchase labels in bulk. If you bought one vintage-dated label for every bottle of a new release, each time a customer requested a custom label (military service logo, law school logo, Pullman Cougar label etc.) or you use a house brand label, it would replace a vintage-dated label on that bottle of wine, resulting in a wasted label from that particular vintage. For example, on average I would have thrown away the labels from 10% of my wines because 10% of my production was ultimately sold with a custom label of some sort.

Making Labels More Versatile: a Cost Saver

Remember that the costs mentioned in my examples were current in 2011, but may not be correct in 2019.

Naturally, there will be times when you don't wish to purchase large orders of one label. No problem! Labels can be purchased in any quantity. Self-adhesive labels purchased in quantities of 1,000 or less and cost about $0.49 each. This average printing cost is above and beyond the one-time costs of creating a label (i.e., artist time, die charges for label stock, foil applications, and label or formula approval costs). The same self-adhesive label mentioned above, purchased at 5,000 units, costs $0.37 each, and in quantities of 10,000 units, the same label is only $0.18.

If my average label cost per case was between $2.34 ($0.18 per label) to $6.37 ($0.49 per label), then the discarded labels would raise my average label cost per case by $0.36 to $0.98 (twelve bottles + box). When the distributor's mark-up and the store's mark-up are figured in, the consumer sees a price increase of between $0.05 and $0.16 per bottle. Winery profit on every 1,000 sold will decline by $360 to $980. A simpler way to think of it is that for every $1 of added per case production cost, the result is a $0.16 increase in the shelf price of a bottle of wine.

Discounts from the printer are based on your total order size

Of course, it is unlikely that a start-up winery can take advantage of most bulk discounts on one label. A start-up winery will almost never use 10,000 copies of a single label. No problem! Printers offer quantity discounts on the total labels purchased in any one order, provided that the label die size does not change—and die sizes are a very important factor for your labels. You pay your label printer for a label die that is used to cut label blanks from self-adhesive roll stock before your labels can be printed. If you change your label die size, then you have to pay for a new die to cut label blanks.

Label prices can vary, but the ratio of printing costs to printing quantity is pretty much fixed. Provided that you do not change the label die size, you can aggregate multiple labels into one order, but you will be charged a small amount for changing labels within an order. These fees are invoiced as "color changed" or "copy changed" and will usually average about $50 apiece. So, to get the best value on label printing, plan to order the maximum number of labels of the same size that you can afford.

Label Size Related to Label Application

Use labels that are of a width and height that fits ALL your bottle sizes: your wine bottle—salsa bottle—jelly jar; it makes no difference what the product is; salsa mild, salsa hot, tomatillo salsa; as long as they are going into the same size jars. By ordering a die to fit the width of your smallest diameter wine bottle—and sticking to this one size—you will save on die charges and maximize label-printing discounts. A label width that is fine for a 750 ml bottle will overlap itself if used on a 375 ml bottle. Your planned label height should take into account the fact that burgundy and hock bottles have a shorter surface than claret bottles. The same height concerns also apply to 375 ml bottles as compared to 750 ml bottles of any shape.

A labeling option you may be tempted to try is gold foil. Foils on wine labels are not only expensive but also require a die to be created for each specific shape and size of image that is to be foiled. A viable and cheaper option is to use gold ink on your labels. That said, the cost of foil, if used judiciously, can be justified by the label's increased eye appeal.

Buy the Artist Rights

When designing their labels, many wineries work with a graphic artist. If you go down this road, you need to understand artist rights. Artist rights mean an artist retains full ownership of the image he or she creates for your label, but you can possibly negotiate the buying of these ownership rights from the artist. In this case, you will be buying ownership rights for the specific image created for your labels. An image is a piece of intellectual property that can be sold or not sold, separate from the physical object (e.g., painting, sketch, or drawing) that you hold in your hand. This typically requires a separate document, ideally on the artist's letterhead, that proves the artist has sold you not only the right to use the image, but also the actual ownership of it.

Packaging equipment

When I started my winery, all I could afford was the least expensive labeling equipment, so I was applying adhesive to the labels and labels to the bottle, one at a time. Balance, remember? This is when I learned about the fine points of label paper thickness, grain direction and adhesives. The adhesive and label size had to match with the labeling machine. When I could afford to upgrade my labeling system years later, the same interactive issues applied.

Do My Own In-House Label Printing and Save a Fortune!

You may be thinking you can dodge the problem of buying large numbers of labels by getting one of the new in-house label printers. One of these machines might work for you, but here is a caution. Some in-house label printers use one toner cartridge that includes black, yellow, blue and magenta inks (as of the available technology in 2011). So far so good; what if your label doesn't use up the four tones colors at the same rate? You end up buying a $200 replacement cartridge because you ran out of a single color of ink. A good in-house laser printer will run about $11,000 with a printing cost of about $0.10 per label. This may be a good option for you, but understand that the cost of the machine must be figured into your total labeling cost.

In order to make up the difference between in-house label costs—$0.10 per label plus the per-label cost to buy the machine—and the average cost for large-run outsourced label printing—with bulk labels at $0.20 each—you must use more than 8,461 cases worth of labels ($11,000 divided by thirteen labels per case). Additionally, you must determine how many years it will take you to amortize your in-house machine given your annual label use rate (i.e., at 2,000 labels per year you amortize your machine in five years, assuming that it lasts with no repair costs). Remember, you must always look at winemaking options based on their purchase, operating, and shipping costs and not just their operating costs.

Packaging on Other Than Glass Bottles

I've written about wine bottles and wine labels. The same concepts and problems relate to other forms of packaging. I also put wine jelly in jars and champagne vinegar in other types of bottles.

Tamper resistant packaging

In designing the labels for my jelly jars, I chose a shape that overlapped the jar lid and sealed on the sides of the jar. My customer had a visible indication that no one had tampered with the contents of the jar. If you choose to use screw-top closure on any packaging, the screw top lid, when applied, has a perforated seal ring press-fit to the glass. This ring is broken when you first twist off the screw top. This is tamper resistance.

Boxes

I used custom-made wood gift boxes for certain items. I designed the boxes to be cheap and easy to build so the unit cost of a gift box of wine stayed price-worthy. I found that hot-branding the wood box was better looking, more durable and cheaper than paper or plastic labels that required hand application. For glass items, I now used glossy coated cardboard boxes that are shipped and stored flat. There are lots of good, available options for gift boxes or bags; just try to choose things that will work for more than one product. Fewer things to store and less costly, as paper boxes are always sold in minimum quantities.

Conclusions

Unless you are making products in bulk, all the aspects of your packaging must work together to look good for the customer. Check with the applicable regulatory agencies to determine what information is mandatory on your packaging. Try to standardize packaging because that minimizes purchase, equipping, and storage issues. Even if it's only once, find a packaging expert and get started right.

15. Equipment Purchase: Strategy and Balance

General business points:
- **Sourcing and adapting equipment**

When I learned winemaking as an apprentice hose dragger, my mentor taught me to spend my equipment dollars wisely.

Perhaps the oldest joke in the wine business is, "How do you make a small fortune in the wine business?"

Answer: "Start with a large fortune!"

Folks who work in the wine industry will often politely smile at this joke, but it's no laughing matter for those at many young wineries. I've seen too many start-up operations spend their money on what they wanted rather than what they needed.

What Can I Adapt to My Needs?

In order to make intelligent equipment purchases, you must understand and think in production units. As mentioned previously, a production unit is all of the neck foils, bottles, corks, and labels needed to produce your wine from one ton of grapes. How many production units can I afford for my first crush? Then how many will I anticipate doing in 2 years—5 years, and will today's equipment purchase be adequate then?

There are many ways to save money on winemaking equipment. You can look for used items and thereby save the immediate depreciation that we are all familiar with when we think about buying cars. Or possibly you could rent the needed equipment locally.

As a winemaker, you must have the use of certain pieces of equipment but you do not necessarily need to own that equipment. Examples: You need to unload pallets of glass from delivery trucks. You need the use of a forklift. Can you order a truck with a lift gate and instead of a forklift use a pallet jack? Or, can you rent or borrow a forklift for two hours? Buying anything that you occasionally use is the least preferable of your options.

Stainless steel (SS) is the industry standard for wine equipment and it can be expensive. But sometimes, more common and less expensive materials can perform the same function as stainless steel. Some materials such as food-grade flexible plastic tubing and schedule forty or schedule eighty PVC pipe with standard barbed-hose fittings are suitable for winemaking. Other materials, such as aluminum or steel that is not rated as stainless, must be avoided. Standard plastic ball and socket hose fittings or barbed fittings commonly found in home and garden stores are also a cost-effective alternative to more expensive SS tri-clamp (TC) fittings.

Remember when using plastics that you want to only use those marked as "food grade." Food grade plastics are made for use in potable water systems and are made without harmful chemicals that can leach out when contacted by the solvent quality of alcohol.

Old dairy tanks, oil tanks, beer kegs or fifty-five-gallon soda-fountain syrup drums are all fine for use in winemaking. Stainless is stainless and need not have been designed and sold as a wine tank. If it fits your need, either for an open-top fermenter or a closed storage vessel, then use it.

When choosing equipment to adapt, keep in mind the special needs of wine as you evaluate the appropriateness of the equipment. For example, a dairy mixing tank has no need to keep air away from the product. So, does the shape of the dairy tank allow you to either top the liquid or to fill any air space with inert gas? Does the tank have access points sufficient to allow cleaning of the interior surfaces? If the dairy tank does not meet one or more of these options, perhaps it can be adapted by drilling a vent hole that can be stoppered. Maybe it can be retrofitted with a closeable and airtight cover or man-way, which can be ordered from a tank manufacture.

Adapting Plastics

Once again, understand that I'm talking about food grade plastic. My keys have just been to buy plastics that were either specified for "potable water" or to reuse drum surpluses from shipping foods. You'll see these drums in various sizes and configurations at home and garden stores. Some of these containers are new, manufactured for use with potable water. Others are surplus from the food packing or processing industry. Used food-grade plastic drums are plentiful, cheap, easy to clean, and easy to store.

The second caution when using plastic is the drums must not have previously contained a vinegar or brine mixture. Drums once used to ship onions, peppers or some types of olives are not suitable for winemaking.

I had the best luck with two specific groups of food grade plastic shipping containers. There are 55-gallon food grade plastic drums used to ship apple juice concentrate. I used them to transport juice and—with the tops cut off—as fermenters for red wines. The second group of drums I liked came in fifty-eight or sixty-eight gallon sizes and were originally used to ship fruits such as cherries or apricots. These drums were configured with large screw-on lids, akin to giant mayonnaise jars. I used them to transport crushed grapes, as fermenters for small-lot blending, and for short-term storage.

Auctions as a Resource

Watch at auctions for tables and chairs, counters, cash registers, pumps, refrigerated cases, and glass racks. Whatever the auction type, there may be things that will work for you without being shiny and new. I purchased two counters from a failed bakery. I purchased two wine display racks from a wine shop auction. Colleges, hospitals, large corporations, and the General Services Administration (GSA) all have large and diverse auctions on a regular basis. Find out a point of contact for the local federal court bankruptcy trustee and get on their mailing list for bankruptcy asset liquidation auctions. Pallet jacks, forklifts, and other material handling tools come up at different auctions, so check all the options. Don't ignore an opportunity without looking at the list of goods to be auctioned.

Conclusions

Whatever we make, there will be specialized equipment as well as equipment that is common to other businesses. Try not to have capital tied up in seldom-used equipment if you can rent or borrow the item when needed.   Adapt when you can. Example: What's the difference between a marine stainless steel # 8 screw and a stainless #8 screw from Home Depot? About $2.00 per screw. When adapting, make sure that what you are considering for use is suitable; think food grade versus non-food grade plastics.

Watch for auctions. Failed businesses often had good equipment, just bad business plans. Get on notification lists for bankruptcy auctions and with local auction companies.

16.   Oak Barrels

General business points:
- **Techniques**
- **Production cost issues**
- **Floor space**

Okay, you looked at the chapter title and said to yourself, "Skip this one." But suppose you are making cheese, balsamic vinegar, dimension lumber or dyeing cloth for sale or use. The wine examples will be the same in terms of aging and floor space issues. Does your product need a climate-controlled environment for heat or humidity, just like wine?

Oaking Wines

In winemaking, an oak barrel has three basic functions: storing liquid, imparting oak flavoring into wine, and softening the tannins in young wines. If properly maintained, an oak barrel can perform the first and third functions for many years, but the more it is used the less it can perform its second function, imparting oak flavoring. To understand barrels and oak flavoring, think of an oak barrel as if it were an S.O.S brand steel wool soap pad. A new S.O.S pad initially provides generous amounts of soap. As the pad is used more and more, the amount of soap it provides declines. Finally, the pad can provide no more soap, and is replaced. So it is with oak barrels. As a wine barrel is used again and again, the amount of oak flavor that seeps into the wine steadily declines.

How long to Oak?

In a class at UC Davis, I learned the basic rules for oaking wine via barrels. With a new barrel, a desirable level of oak flavor is achieved in 90 days. The second filling of that barrel will now require 6 months of aging to achieve the same degree of oak as you got in 90 days with the new barrel. A third filling of that same barrel again doubles the time from 6 months to 1 year to achieve the same level of oaking in the finished wine.

Tax implications of aging

Wine is taxed by the IRS on a Uniform Capitalization (UCAP) basis rather than on a Cost of Goods Sold basis. Example: The basic difference is that for an article of clothing, when cut and sewn, including overhead for the year produced, the taxable value of the item is fixed. Under UCAP, if a wine is in bulk awaiting bottling at the end of one tax year and then bottled in a later tax year, the taxable value of the wine keeps increasing, as a percentage of your total overhead accrues to the unsold wine every year it is on premises. More about UCAP in a coming chapter.

Seasoning new Cooperage

When your new barrels are delivered, they need to be sterilized and hydrated to prevent leaks. I used a good hot water rinse followed by an immediate cold-water fill to hydrate the wood. All new barrels will leak when first filled, but should seal in a matter of hours. If a leak remains, usually at the bilge point, sprinkle a small amount of food-grade bentonite through the bunghole. The bentonite will settle into the leak between barrel staves, bloom to its full size, and seal the leak from the inside of the barrel.

Avoid Over Oaking

I feel oak barrel aging is often overdone in the United States. We sometimes make wines that are caricatures of fine French wines—too hot, too jammy, too pricey and too much oak. Of course, this is just my opinion.

In most wine regions of France, oak is used with great restraint for flavoring vessels. Older, so-called neutral oak barrels and tanks are more often used for micro-oxygenation to help soften tannins and balance wine structures. This usage model is not primarily concerned with producing noticeable oak tones in their wines. The amount of oaking desired is accomplished by using a small number of new oak barrels to strongly oak small lots of wine that are thereafter blended into the large vintage.

Re-coopering Barrels

My mentor, Tom Kruse, showed me how to re-cooper a barrel by carefully removing the hoops and barrelhead. This takes some skill and patience because there are no nails holding the barrel staves and heads together. I began by re-coopering whiskey barrels that had been sold to home and garden stores as planters. I used a paint scraper to remove any charring and re-expose the oak surface for wine aging.

In 1977, whiskey barrels were selling for $20 each while new American oak wine barrels sold for $120 each. Whiskey barrels and wine barrels are very similar, and a reworked whiskey barrel with the interior char removed will age and influence wine in the same manner as a new oak wine barrel in its second filling.

The only pieces of equipment needed to re-cooper barrels are a hoop driver, a mineral wax sealing putty, a four-pound hammer, and a long-handled paint scraper. The mineral wax, or gate tallow, and the hoop driver are the only specialty items, and these can be obtained through most large winemaking supply houses.

Trade-offs with using older/neutral oak barrels

So, what's the problem with just being patient and aging the wine longer in an older barrel? Nothing! BUT evaporation and space considerations are trade-offs that you will have to weigh.

Shrinkage

Shrinkage by evaporation—a process the French refer to as ullage—is generally about 5 percent per year, unless you've taken on the extra expense of climate-controlled storage for your wine-filled barrels. If you aged wine in barrel for two full years, then you would expect to lose up to 10 percent of your original liquid volume vs. losing about 1 percent in ninety days. That's a lot of valuable finished wine that you'd be losing! Along with the shrinkage, you should also expect slightly increased oxidation. The positive side to the dilemma is the softening of the wine's structure by micro-oxygenation. You'll need to find your balance point for the level of oaking and an acceptable amount of shrinkage, given your own business realities.

Costs involved in oaking with barrels

There is one last potential cost to consider when oaking your wine in barrels. Because the surface of an oak barrel absorbs liquid and retains color, you will need to use separate barrels for red wines and white wines. A red wine can be aged in a barrel that previously held a white wine, but the reverse situation—ageing a white wine in a barrel that previously held red wine—will result in a blush. So, if you are making both red and white wines, you will likely have both increased monetary needs for separate barrels and increased space needs to store those barrels.

As I hope this narrative has a long shelf life, I won't speculate on the future cost of barrels, but will instead give you a formula to use to estimate your barrel costs. The amount of wine that can be barrel-aged in a standard American oak barrel during its three-year life span is 177 gallons. At 2.377 gallons per case, this translates to 74.7 cases of wine. Divide your delivered barrel cost by this number to determine what you are paying to oak your wine. For example, if your delivered barrel cost is $355, the average cost to oak your wine is about $4.75 per case. Remember the multiplier effect, $1 of extra cost equals $0.16 added retail price, so the shelf price of each bottle has been increased by a minimum of $0.75. An added dollar here, one more added there, and pretty soon we're talking about real money.

Floor Space Requirements

The second factor that comes into play with long periods of barrel aging is the increased floor space and barrel racks needed to store the extra barrels. Remember, to get the same amount of oak flavor in a wine, each successive filling of a barrel requires double the aging time of the previous filling—ninety days, then six months, then one year, etc. To illustrate why you'll need extra floor space, let's look at an example showing why barrels are typically replaced after three uses.

An example concerning needed space

Assume you need to oak 1,000 gallons of red wine per year. Suppose that we stack the barrels in two-barrel racks, each stacked three layers high (fifty-nine gallons times six barrels), then you would need three such stacks to barrel age 1,000 gallons in all new barrels. In the second vintage of your barrel's life, the same barrels are available to be refilled and the aging time is increased to six months, so the space footprint of the barrels does not increase from one year to the next.

More space may be needed in year 3

In the third vintage year, you need twelve months barrel aging time to get the desired level of oaking, so your space footprint may or may not change. The variables here are where and in what did you ferment and fine your wine. You will be teetering on the edge of not having barrel space when you need it—assuming you can financially afford to barrel age your wines for a year before offering them for sale. Now apply the actual timing of production to the third year example and look for possible problems.

The grape crush in your region takes place over a ten-week period, start to finish. You are working with multiple varieties of grapes, both reds and whites; some ripen early and others ripen late. (My example uses named months, such as September, October and November. You can substitute numbers for names, such as month one, month two.) You crush 7.25 tons of fruit in late September and begin to ferment the must in open-top fermenters containing 1150 gallons of juice. Fermentation, after a brief pre-soak, takes eight days and you press out your raw wine on October 1st. The Syrah is moved into variable capacity SS tanks and given a gelatin fining. On November 1st, your wine is heat stable, and you put it into barrels. After twelve months of barrel age you are ready to bottle this wine.

Life's curve-balls that you might see

Are you likely to have any of the following problems? You want to produce 1000 gallons of Syrah and you plan on having 1000 gallons of barrel space freed up by bottling wine from year 2 of your barrel cycle. You are still fermenting some wines and don't have time or space to operate your bottling line right then. But you still can't get a mobile bottling truck on site for another month and then you're into the Christmas season and need to be working your tasting room. You didn't have space, or space and money, to have previously brought in 480 cases of empty glass. You have another time commitment that doesn't permit you to bottle your Syrah on the first day it's ready. The 1000 gallons of Syrah once removed from barrels has to go into other storage, probably stainless steel. More tankage and floor space are thus required. Based on your average monthly sales of Syrah you need to bring this most recent vintage to market with less than twelve months oaking or less than a minimum of three months bottle aging (to get over bottle shock).

Fourth year it hits the fan

In the fourth year of your production cycle you will now need to increase the number of barrels, racks, and floor space needed for barrel aging! Of course, there are strategies that might reduce the impact of the ever-doubling barrel age times, such as mixing and rotating older barrels with new barrels, but you cannot get around the need for increased floor space. Your barrels have reached the point where they are considered neutral and unable to impart oak flavor into your wine.

There is a definite spiral of diminishing returns on oak flavoring and increased need for space if you choose to fill your barrels beyond the optimum three vintage barrel cycles. There are ways you can reuse some of those barrels. Do like the French; keep and differentially use oak barrels. You have a few new barrels for imparting oak flavors and neutral barrels for micro-oxygenation. So, if you choose to oak your wines in barrels, add the cost of barrel aging into your mental data banks along with a maximum of three fillings for each new barrel.

Conclusions

Cost of goods sold versus UCAP? Does the flooring of an unfinished product change how the item is taxed in your industry? Do any of your procedures force you to increase your floor space? Think about if your product can be produced more efficiently through use of an alternative production method. Here again, it's all about finding the best balance in time, space and money.

17. Oak Alternatives

Just like I looked for alternatives to buying new or specialty equipment, the same frugality can apply to some components. I say some, because as I've said before, "You can make bad wine out of good grapes, but you can't make good wine out of bad grapes." Or, as my bookie/bootlegger father might say, "You can't make chicken salad out of chicken shit." Beware of misplaced, false economies!

Oak Alternatives

The first option for oaking your wine is to use the French system of blending wine from neutral barrels with a small amount of heavily oaked wine from new barrels. If you choose this strategy, do blending trials to discover the blending ratios that achieve your desired degree of oak.

Oak alternatives will reduce the cost of oaking by about ninety percent. There are several types of oak alternatives: chips, oak powder, cubes, staves and rods. Some of these are loose-packed items while others are bagged or strung together to allow for standard dosing units.

When creating my wines, I have used oak chips and oak powder, (basically oak sawdust) to augment barrel aging. Oak powder is added to the fermenters. I put mine in during a pre-soak period on red grapes. Oak chips, on the other hand, are put into the finished wine during aging.

If you are using stainless steel tanks, rows of small oak staves can be placed around the interior circumference of your tank. Oak barrels can be rejuvenated using this same system.

Considerations in Choosing Between Alternatives

When choosing oak alternatives there are two basic considerations: ease of insertion/removal and needed quantity. With regards to insertion and removal, you can dump loose chips into a barrel through the bunghole and get the chips back out the same way. But once you've discovered the difficulty of removing chips from a barrel you may not want to do it again. If you are using neutral oak barrels, then strings of oak strips or cubes roped together work better than loose chips for insertion and removal.

Oaking in plastic vessels

I switched my oak aging procedure to use plastic, cube-shaped wine tanks instead of oak barrels. These plastic tanks are produced by a U.S. company under the name Flextank. They have a sixteen-inch top opening that allows the use of bagged oak chips. For my wines, I placed a mesh bag of chips in the 300-gallon cube and then filled the tank with wine. Because the tank surface does not absorb liquid you do not need to have separate barrels for reds or whites as is necessary with oak barrels. If the tank does not completely fill with wine, then you must introduce inert gas into the ullage (empty) space to prevent oxidation. Before finding a source for pre-bagged chips, I used the same basic method by placing loose chips into nylon mesh bags that were sourced from home winemaking supply firms.

Timing issues

The second major factor in using oak alternatives is dosage—getting all the oak you want but not too much. I determined my dosage by reviewing recommended immersion times from each vendor. Surface-to-volume ratios are all-important when it comes to alternative oaking. How much oak surface is being exposed in what volume of liquid for how long? Each vendor will have a recommended immersion time based on the quantity of product used and volume of wine being oaked.

My oak alternatives timing formulas

There's no magic formula for how much or how long to oak, but here is a list of what you need to focus on to make the alternatives work in your particular situation. Take good notes!

I used oak powder at the rate of one and one-half pounds of powder per ton of grapes during fermentation. For oak chips, I used one twenty-five pound bag in three hundred gallons of wine for ninety days. Think of oak like seasoning food; you do it to taste. Remember, the perceived oak in wine seems to increase with bottle age, so the oak flavor should be at a medium acceptable level when you remove the oak from contact with the wine. The same caution of not over-oaking goes for barrels, too. A little oak enhances the flavor of wine, while a lot of oak can create distraction and overwhelm the fruit. That said, go with what your audience wants and then adjust to find the preference of your own market.

Conclusions

Search for production methods or material alternatives that are money savers without compromising quality. If your industry presents such opportunities, then thoroughly test the alternative, taking notes, to find the best timing and equipment pairings to realize fully the potential cost and/or time savings. Remember that everything in a method, timing-equipment-material, must be integrated to work together.

18. Keep Extra Key Parts

General business points:
- **Avoiding down time**
- **Keeping source data on suppliers**

While learning winemaking as a hobbyist in one of northern California's many wine regions, I noticed the two wineries where I apprenticed would both borrow equipment from, and loan equipment to, neighboring wineries. The same was true for lending or selling supplies such as filter pads, empty bottles, or unbranded corks. The wineries viewed themselves as part of a community so they helped the other members of that community, even though, on some level, they were helping a competitor.

In 1981, I moved to the wilds of northern Idaho, more than 100 miles from the nearest winery. It seemed nice to be the only winery around, but it also meant I had no community of winemakers from which to borrow, and no winemaking equipment stores or winery supply stores nearby.

Availability of Parts/Supplies to Buy or Borrow

Everything I needed equipment-wise came from out-of-state, so I quickly learned that when buying a non-perishable item, buy two instead of one. Filling my immediate need and having a spare part gave me a wonderful feeling of confidence. Stocking spare parts prevents or minimizes the impact and lost time if something breaks during a time-sensitive operation such as crushing or bottling. I also learned to keep the part number and source information for each part. When it came time to reorder, I knew the who, what, and where of what I needed.

Back-up Equipment

To create backup options, I kept my hobbyist gear when I upgraded to small-scale commercial equipment. When I bought a used semi-automatic corker, I kept my floor-model hand corker as a backup. When I got a used motorized must pump with stainless-steel cart and remote-control capacity, I saved my hand-operated bellows type must pump as a backup. The same was true for transfer pumps and hoses when I went from hobby size to small commercial size. Remember, if you own something and it is not broken, keep it. It just might have utility or monetary value in the future.

Conclusions

Plan ahead so that your production schedule is as protected from downtime as possible. Whatever you are making, you've got orders to fill and customers who want product, not excuses. It may not matter to your customer that your production delay was unplanned, especially if they have a time-dependent need and/or other sourcing alternatives.

19. The Honeymoon

General business points:
- **Novelty**

There is a honeymoon period for each new winery when their first release sells out quickly. This phenomenon is not dependent on the quality of your product or the high value of your wine. Instead, the honeymoon period is a function of your being a novelty. Novelty and initial interest are opportunities to acquire customers for life. Plus, the initial sales are a wonderful validation of your dream! Just don't make the mistake of thinking, "Wow, I'm good, and my sales are always going to be like this. I think I'll need an unlisted phone number and no signage just to manage the crowds."

You will be a novelty until you are not a novelty. When that time comes is controlled by your customers and other competitors, not by you. If you started small, a significant percentage of your early sales may be made to family and friends. You will also make sales to folks who are just curious about your wines. The family-and-friends sales will last longer than the sales to the curious. If anyone likes your wines, then hopefully they will be back. But expect that the shelf life of significant sales to family and friends will subside. To be successful on a sustained basis you must transition to selling to the general public.

20. "Cache Phloe" Wines

General business points:
- **Production time**
- **Availability strategies**
- **Which wines to produce**

Years ago, there was a TV commercial for the now-gone Paul Masson Winery, featuring the famous actor Orson Wells. Clad in a smoking jacket, glass of wine in hand, he looked to the camera and said. "At Paul Masson we'll sell no wine before its time." Cut to images of wine cellars, huge casks and dusty bottles.

Our industry joke was a follow-up question to Orson: "So, how do you know when it's time?

The punch line is, "Your accountant will tell you when it's time. Get that shit out of here. Let it age on the truck."

As the owner of a new winery, your biggest initial obstacle may be monetary. Fortunately, there are a number of strategies and options you can apply to increase the cash flow in your winery.

Production Time

Not surprisingly, some wonderful wines take a long time to produce and an even longer time to age before they become saleable; other delicious wines have a shorter production time. Obviously, the wines with a shorter production period allow you to enjoy a quicker return on your investment. For many small wineries, the variable production times present a conundrum. Do they produce a large quantity of white and pink wines, which take less time than red wines? Do they produce fruit and honey wines that take even less time to become marketable than white grape wines? Do they have enough time, space, and money to focus on making big, monster red wines, even though these wines are the slowest to come to market? These are questions you will have to answer when starting your winery.

Strategies

If circumstances require you to sell your wines before they are ready—keep in mind that wine often tastes ordinary and lackluster until that magic moment when it transforms into an outstanding wine—then you have two choices to speed your wines along: blending or selling wine futures.

Blending

The Tax and Trade Bureau (TTB) rules allow you to market wine as "produced" or "made" by your winery if the wine content is at least seventy-five percent your own. This means you can buy and blend in a percentage of bulk wine that may, by its addition, make your own wine ready to sell at an earlier date than originally expected. If you need to blend, do blending trials before buying or doing the actual batch blend. If your blending trials require you to blend in more than 25% of the total finished liquid volume, no problem. However, your label for the blended batch, to be legal, must avoid using the terms "Made or Produced by…" and substitute "Blended or Vinted by…"

Wine futures

Your other option is selling wine futures. Think of a commodity exchange where a buyer is speculating that buying an item now at a reduced price will create an economic advantage at a later date. Example: "This Cabernet is going to be fabulous in another two years, but if you buy today, you'll save forty percent off the future release price." In this way you can trade future profits for cash flow now.

Which Wines to Produce

Before you ever run into the issue of blending wines or selling wine futures, you will have to make a decision on which wines to produce. A number of factors, including the balance of time and space, come into play here. Your decisions about which types of wines to create can be some of the most complex decisions you will have to make.

What will get to the market faster: Reds or Whites?

Despite the fact that red wines take the longest to become saleable, dry red wines are the easiest wines to make because of their reduced need for filtration. Dry red wines have no residual sugar to re-ferment in the bottle, and the pigment will cover some minor sins in clarity or oxidation. White wines and pink wines, on the other hand, require better oxygen management and mistakes are more apparent.

Additionally, non-red wines are usually served chilled, and chilling grape juice causes a natural element of the juice—potassium bi-tartrate—to come out of solution in the form of small salt-like crystals. These crystals, or *wine jewels*, are harmless. Wines that will be served chilled require cold stabilization to remove the potassium bi-tartrate crystals from the finished product. The average American consumers don't want spots on their apples—even if they know that no spots means pesticides likely were applied—and don't want harmless crystals in their wine. They perceive these particles as flaws. Check any white bulk wine you buy for cold stability so you get no big surprises.

Fining options to shorten production/maturing time

You can finesse the aging delay to some degree by making your wines in different manners and different varieties. For example, fining agents allow you to sacrifice either tannin or color. Gelatins, as well as other types of protein fining agents, remove some tannin from your wines. Different grape varieties have different tannin structures, as well as containing differences in other astringent tasting phenolic compounds—in other words, different grape varieties result in different aging times. These points are not either/or choices but are instead interactive elements for you to consider.

Making what the market demands

Sometimes you may be forced to make certain varieties or styles that are less profitable but in great demand by the public. I made and sold a blush that was the least profitable of all my wines. But if I did not have this option, a portion of the customers would have walked out without ever sampling my other wine options. Instead, I got them to stay in my tasting room by offering a blush wine. This, in turn, meant I had the chance to sell them something else by approaching the customer with a comment such as "If you like Blush, then you might also like a lightly sweet Riesling or Gewürztraminer." The same technique will work in your shop with any number of wines.

Don't Sacrifice Future Continuity of Supply in Your Haste

And finally, you must also consider which grape varieties you can acquire on a ready and sustained basis. Distributors and stores want to know that after they develop a market for your wine, there will be continual access to that wine. To validate this need for continuity of supply, ask yourself how many times you've seen a note on a store shelf or a restaurant wine list that reads, "Joe Smith's Dynamite Red: Back in six months." I'm betting you've never seen such a note. Merchants always fill empty spaces with other products.

Conclusions

Unless you are lucky enough to be the only game in town, with no competitors for your product line, you must acknowledge your customers' need for continuity of supply. Your sales channels work hard to develop recognition for particular items. It hurts you in the long term if you can't be a reliable source. Once you are dropped from a merchant's line for being unreliable, it is almost impossible to reclaim your spot.

An example: there was a microbrewery in my town that made good beer; so good in fact that they couldn't supply the demand. Lacking capitalization to expand and meet the demand, their available supply was insufficient to meet cash flow needs, and they went out of business after two years. The point is we worry that no one will buy our product while not seeing the risk that if everyone buys our product, we can't keep up.

21. Continuity of Supply

General business points:
- **Production lead time**

I used to worry about not being successful—that no one would buy my wine. But believe it or not, there is an unanticipated consequence of being too successful. Having wine that no one wants is obviously a problem. So, too, is not being able to supply your customers.

Your wine production must be planned in such a way as to be a reliable source. The best way to accomplish this is to track the rate at which your individual wines sell. This allows you to know approximately when you need to make or buy more of a particular item.

Understanding Production Time

Maintain continuity of supply.

If your "Faux Pas Red" sells at the rate of twenty cases per month and you have two hundred cases on hand in January, you have a ten-month supply which will last through the end of November. If you are buying bulk wine for your "Faux Pas Red," you need to figure in the time needed to obtain and bottle this bulk wine; usually about one month. You'll also need to allow time for your newly bottled wines to rest—a minimum of two months—to get over bottle shock. Using this example, and working backwards from October, you'll need to acquire your bulk wine in July in order to make it available for sale in October, which is when your two hundred cases are expected to be gone.

If, instead of buying bulk wine, you are making your "Faux Pas Red," then you must allow more lead time. When can you get the grapes you'll need? If you can only get your grapes in October, then you'll need to add the number of months between when you'll run out of your current stock and when you can get grapes for new stock to the actual production time for that wine. How long from fermenter to barrel (four months), barrel to bottle

83

(six months), finished wine to saleable wine (twelve months)? All of these questions must be taken into account.

In my small winery, red wines required a minimum of twelve months of bottle-aging time. My basic production cycle for red wines required a two-year lead time with a production run consisting of a three-year supply. If I released my 2007 Faux Pas Red in August 2009, I had to make enough wine to last until my next vintage would be ready, which included the number of months until grapes were available, the amount of production time, and a built-in cushion against unanticipated delays or increased demand.

Example on Figuring Time

You have a total annual production capacity for grape wines of two thousand gallons. Keep in mind the lessons of production lead time and rate of sales. This is called depletion. You should not divide your product line into more wines than you can produce and still meet your average annual needs. Do the math and decide if you can make one wine, four wines, eight wines, etc. Remember, you can make more varieties of wine by extending your product season—honey wines in January and fruit wines in July—just as long as your floor space and available time allows for increased inventory.

Finally, all the concerns that I've explained about being a reliable supplier for your wholesale customers also apply to keeping your own tasting room supplied with product. However, it is more important to keep your wholesale customers stocked with wine. At least in the tasting room you can temporarily offer customers a substitute.

Conclusions

Whatever you make must be sold, perhaps multiple times at different levels of the customer chain. You've spent time and money advertising, building a distribution network, and establishing a reputation with customers. You do not want to have your reputation be one of unreliability. Continuity of supply is vital to keeping customers.

22. Distributors: The Good, the Bad and the Ugly

General business points:
- **Large and small distributors**
- **How they price wine**
- **Store resets**

Remember balance? Time-space-money. Unless you have time and money to be your own sales and delivery force, you'll need to operate in a three-tiered system: producer-distributor-retailer. You'll pay for the distributer's services by sharing your profits, but is that cheaper than trying to do it yourself? It was for me.

Big Guys

Distributors are the guys who buy your wines and then resell those wines to retail accounts such as stores and restaurants. In general, there are two basic types of distributors. There are large, regional distributorships that often feature warehouse operations in several states. And there are small, specialty house distributorships that often handle imported wines, imported beers, microbrews or smaller boutique types of wines.

I've previously explained how supermarkets allot shelf space, and their concerns about profitability and turn-over. This is difficult to avoid when you are sharing shelves with some national brands. Certain national brands whose names I dare not mention for fear of legal action will often tell a distributor to "Sell XXX number of cases per month or we'll go to your competitor." If your distributor faces the choice of allocating good spots to their cash cow—a national brand with a national marketing program—or to the little local guy, who do you think they'll choose? A distributor's existence might depend on meeting their sales quota, so while they may like you and like your wines, their economic future is not linked to your success. Be realistic. To them, you are optional.

Remember that the major distributor who sells national advertised brands must fill sales quotas. They put the wines that must sell to meet a quota in the best positions. The little guy gets what space is left; think bottom shelves.

The big guy kiss off

The large distributorships are generally representatives for national brands of both beer and wine. If you are small in size, no matter how good your wines are, you will probably hear the line, "We're worried that you may not be able to supply all the wine we'll need if we take you on." When you hear this, you have officially been kissed off. This is distributor code for "We're not interested, but we don't want to offend you, so we use this line instead."

Little Guys

I have found the specialty distributorships to be service-based and more likely to be more suited to a small winery. In order to survive, a small distributorship must find value in your products before they will take you on. They will not purchase your wines unless they believe you will improve their product line. For example, you might fill a price niche, or you might represent a winemaking or grape-growing region that is under-represented in their product line. But as with any distributor, expect to share the cost of samples they provide to customers. Try to support your distributors with information and point-of-sale materials such as shelf talkers, copies of news releases concerning recent awards, etc. Whatever makes it easier for them to sell your wine will benefit you both.

How Distributors Price Wine

In the Mark-Up section to follow, you will read about distributor's mark-up as a percentage on cost. Their price is based on their total cost to resell your wines. This includes the cost of your wine as purchased by the distributor, any state taxes they must remit, and the cost of getting your wines to their warehouse. When you are courting a distributor, remember they evaluate your goods in terms of salability and price point in their market. What may be an excellent price in your tasting room may not be a good price on the store shelf. Their willingness to represent you is based on the quality of your goods and on their ability to sell it in a competitive market.

Store Resets

Some stores, especially supermarkets, assign particular shelves to individual distributors. They may even assign wines from an individual distributor to an exact shelf space or bin spot. Other stores do not assign wine spaces, so distributors repeatedly jockey for the best spots. Prime spots are end displays, refrigerated cases, and shelf space that is waist high or above. As a small winery in a store that doesn't assign spaces, you are in for the "reset shuffle" where your products may end up on the bottom shelves or in other less desirable spaces.

A strategy for avoiding the reset shuffle

The only dependable method I've found to avoid the reset shuffle is to develop a special relationship with the store. This approach often guaranteed me a good shelf spot. How do you make yourself special to the store? Try offering regular in-store tastings, custom label services such as personalized messages for special orders, a house brand labeling program (if permissible in your state), or co-promotions of your wines with other store departments. Before offering store branding or custom labels, research state laws to discover if there are restrictions on these practices. And never cheat on the state's rules. They will bite you, your distributor, and, worst of all, the store for which you cheated. Remember, you get just one chance to get a vendor in trouble.

As an example of co-promotion within a store, you provide wine tasting in conjunction with the store's meat department, featuring wines that pair well with the store's sausage, barbecued meats, etc. You can also co-promote with the bakery department to show how your dessert wines pair with the bakery's chocolates or wedding cakes. There is no limit to how you can co-promote, but remember that you are attempting to create value for your wines by supporting an item that the store currently offers.

Conclusions

Access to the market is key. At the time and place I started, distributors were necessary because I could not afford a sales and delivery force. This may not be a problem for you if you ship by rail or other common carrier, such as a trucking company. Or, you may be able to ship via UPS, DHL or FedEx, if your product fits their size limits. In any case, know the totality of your market, the cost of distribution and its effect on your price and the ultimate retail price.

23. Setting Your Price

General Business Points:
- **Merchant mark-up**
- **Adjusting your price**
- **State laws**
- **House accounts**
- **Price increases**
- **Expanding distribution**
- **State dispensaries**
- **Shipping cost and retail price**

There was a Northern California winery that reportedly set the price for each new release by comparing it side-by-side with a famous and expensive French wine of the same type. They figured if the French could get X-number of dollars for a bottle, then their wine could be priced according to its relative quality. I think the name of this winery was "Chateau Les Ego," but memory fails me. I considered selling my wine for $1,000 per bottle. That way I didn't have to sell very many bottles. After all, my wine was that good. How did I know? I asked my Mom (stated with tongue firmly in cheek).

Know the Merchant Mark-up and Applicable State Laws

The store mark-up will usually be in the range of twenty-five percent to fifty percent. Typically, restaurants mark-up wines based on cost plus one hundred percent to two hundred percent. A simple way to think of how much markup is involves is that the restaurant will fix its price for a single serving of any wine at what they paid for the entire bottle. Finding out the markup of an individual restaurant, store, or distributor will allow you to determine the price points you must hit in order to sell directly to those markets. Most states require you to sell any particular wine to all outlets in their state at the same wholesale price. If this is the case, sometimes your wine will just not fit within a particular merchant's pricing scheme.

Adjusting Prices to Better Fit Your Market

Suppose you want a particular wine to sell at the approximate price of similar wines. You set your prices by posting them with each state's liquor authority. You can do this when you release a new vintage of any wine. Also, most states allow you, at pre-set intervals, to repost an adjusted price.

Hitting a retail price point

By talking to my distributors and using them as consultants, I developed a system for setting my prices in a three-tiered system. It allowed me to control my wines' retail prices in stores. If you plan to sell both retail and wholesale, you need to understand multilevel pricing.

My system used the average price of comparable wine in the market place and calculated the average mark-up taken by stores and distributors as factors in setting my wholesale prices. The system works backwards from the retail shelf or wine list price.

First, determine the average price for comparable wines in local stores. Then, subtract from the retail price the average mark-up added by the store, and the mark-up added by the distributor on his sale to the store. Example: One bottle of Merlot retails for $10. The average store mark-up is thirty percent, so working backward the store could pay the distributor no more than $7.70 per bottle of Merlot ($10 divided by 1.30). The distributor marks up the wine thirty percent, so if he sold it for $7.70 to the store, he purchased the wine from the producer for $5.91 ($7.70 divided by 1.30).

The Danger of trying to get too big

One of the most painful things I've repeatedly observed in the wine business occurs when a small winery attempts to expand into the wholesale market. Many small wineries start out exclusively with direct retail sales. The pain they experience at the thought of dropping their prices so far from retail in order to make their wine viable in a three-tier wholesale system is excruciating to watch. These wineries would have been well served to have a production cost analysis done prior to selling any wine. The analysis would have anticipated the realities of wholesale and retail distribution—and saved them a lot of pain!

State Laws: Educate Yourself!

Different states have different regulations, so you should research the rules for each state's liquor control board. I've found state liquor control staff to be very willing to give help and information. Expect to post your wholesale prices for retail accounts and/or distributors with state alcohol authorities. You may be required to enter into exclusive contracts with a single distributor or have only one distributor in a particular area. Expect to be required to send the distributor a written notice of price changes and a written notice if you wish to discontinue your relationship with that distributor.

House Accounts

Some states give you the ability to sell directly to licensed retailers. Having direct sales accounts, also known as house accounts, in the same town represented by one of your distributors may undercut your distributor's posted prices. You must often make a choice between using house accounts and retaining a distributor. Because of my business longevity, I was occasionally able to maintain distributor representation and house accounts in the same town. When this overlapping of sales efforts worked, it worked because of rules I applied to my own sales. If you're selling directly to stores, then you become responsible for any state excise or liquor taxes that distributors pay at the time of sale.

First, I allowed any of my house accounts to become distributor accounts if they so desired. When this occurred, it was usually for reasons of convenience. A local distributor could typically deliver product more promptly than I could. I delivered free-of-charge to house accounts within a seventy-five mile radius of the winery, but I only made these free deliveries one time per month. Second, any account opened by a distributor was their exclusive account. Third, I kept any accounts where I did regular business in custom labels for stores. I kept these accounts so that a distributor did not have to stock multiple labelings of the same wine. Using these three rules would often be enough to gain and retain a distributor's business in an area where I kept some house accounts. It pays to be nice to your distributors.

Price Increases are Geometric not Arithmetic

Remember there is a geometric effect to your price increase when the wine reaches the consumer. Adding $1 to your delivered (delivered to distributor, warehouse or your wholesale customer) cost per case returns only $0.08 per bottle to you, but this increases the final shelf price by about $0.16 per bottle, or roughly double. So imagine adding an extra $1 per bottle profit because your wine is that just darn good. Now, add $1 per case for shipping/warehousing and another $1 per bottle for fancier packaging. These three increases together raise your case price by $25, which raises the shelf price of your wine about $4.00 per bottle. This may not be an issue if you are selling ultra-premium wine, but it will be an issue if you are trying to sell wines in any of the other categories—jug, fighting varietal, or premium.

Pitfalls to Expanding Your Distribution

One key obstacle to increasing your distribution is the multiplier effect at the distributor and retailer levels that raises the shelf price of your product dramatically. What was a price-worthy wine in your tasting room or in your local market may not be price competitive across the state when shipping expense is added. Two Buck Chuck did well in your area because it cost $3 per bottle! If the same wine had been priced at $6 to cover the increased cost of shipping your wine across the state, I doubt it would have been such a phenomenal seller.

Many distributors do not want to store large amounts of your wines and will therefore require you to utilize a bonded warehouse in their area. The cost of bonded storage after the wine leaves your winery is your expense. Remember, it's not how much money you make, but how much you get to keep! Now let's take the same $10 Merlot that we discussed previously.

The Effect of Shipping on Your Retail Price

So, let's say you are selling a wine at $5.91 per bottle wholesale, and your per case profit is $36. Now add to that a shipping cost of $12 per case, which gives your out-of-town distributor a laid-in cost of $6.91 per bottle ($12 per case shipping, or $1 per bottle shipping, plus your original price of $5.91 per bottle). Warehousing costs, as of this writing, run about $1 per case per month. Let's suppose you average three months storage per case, which means your price to the distributor has necessarily gone up again: now to $7.16 per bottle. Remember that the distributor may also be adding on its own state's excise tax, so we'll use a modest $2 per case tax figure for this example. With the cost of excise tax added on, the distributor's profit will now be figured at an on-cost base of $7.33 per bottle. The store must now pay the distributor $9.53 per bottle, and the retail price on the store shelf will go from $10 to about $12.48. So, shipping and storage had an aggregated net effect of raising the price to the consumer by about 25%.

You must decide if this change in price point will be adverse or neutral to the sales of your wine. Also remember that if you are a small producer, you are probably targeting specialty markets, wine shops, and restaurants where average mark-ups at the retail level will be 50 to 100 percent. Your hometown restaurant would have a wine list price of $20 on your wine while the out-of-town restaurant will be selling the same bottle for $25. This compounding effect of increased mark-up due to shipping and storage is something to keep in mind whenever you plan to expand your distribution area.

My own hard lesson: a cautionary tale

One year when I was trying to expand my distribution, I approached a large, multi-state distributor about selling my wines in areas where I currently had no distribution. Having been around for a number of years, my brand was a known quantity in the regional wine industry. The large distributor agreed to take on my brand but only on condition that they acquire all my business in all the areas they serviced. Now I was faced with the choice of dropping a smaller distributor who had faithfully sold my wines in a limited area, or expanding my distribution through the use of the big guy.

This was a price too high. I would not dump a small, loyal partner for the chance to go with a bigger firm. How did I come to this decision? If the mega-distributor didn't sell enough of my wine to meet their expectations, I'd get dumped by Mister Big. Then, because I'd burned my bridge behind me, I couldn't go back to the small, reliable, regional partner whom I had unceremoniously dumped. I decided to stick with the smaller distributor, and I kept that distributor for twenty-eight years, so I suggest that loyalty still has value.

Selling to State Dispensaries

I used to ship wine regularly to the Idaho State Liquor Dispensary (ISLD) warehouse in Boise. The ISLD required all of their wine sources to work on a contract basis guaranteeing ISLD a fixed delivered price with a ninety day lead time for any price increases on my end. Due to the nature of the ISLD, I could never know in advance how many cases they would order, which often led to an issue with shipping costs.

Shipping Costs as a Variable

Shipping costs can vary on a daily basis according to fuel prices. More importantly, motor freight carriers will often limit your floor space within their trucks. Their shipping costs are based on the matrix of size-weight-distance. Consequently, it was more expensive per case for me to ship a shrink-wrapped pallet (SWP) with one layer of cases—twelve or fifteen cases— than it was to ship the same SWP with two or three layers of wine cases on the pallet. The SWP had the same footprint regardless of how many cases of wine it carried. I eventually set my contract price to ISLD based on a twenty-four-case order using $11 per case as the shipping cost. If for some reason ISLD ordered only twelve cases in a single month, I lost about $30 on shipping costs because I still had to pay the shipping based on the SWP floor space. On the other hand, if ISLD placed an order for thirty-six cases, I profited an extra $30.

Conclusions

Being competitive in your market is key. It doesn't matter which competitive strategy you've picked: price, value or quality. We've discussed strategies for limiting production costs while not sacrificing product integrity. This chapter explained that sometimes the only variable that you can control is your profit. Know the mark-up at each level of your distribution chain. Remember, those percentages of profit exert a geometric rather than arithmetic influence on retail prices. Finally, in your zeal to expand sales, remember that it is not how much money you gross, but how much money you net.

24. When Things Go Wrong

General business points:
- **Problem solving**
- **Lawsuits**
- **Net 30 delivery**

In the course of my twenty-eight years of operating a commercial winery, I've been in plenty of unwanted, unplanned, and undesirable situations. This section will give a list of ideas for avoiding problems—and it's all based on my real-life experiences over those same twenty-eight years.

A Businesslike Attitude

First, some general comments and observations about business and business ethics:

Blame

When things go wrong, it is more important to ask, "What can I do to fix this?" than it is to say, "Who can I blame, since I obviously have no responsibility for the current mess?" Blame is a short-term response to what may be a long-term problem. When things go wrong, it is seldom the fault of a lone individual, especially if the problem is rooted in a simple misunderstanding. In times of trouble, it is more productive to seek what can be done to resolve a problem than it is to seek a party on which to fix the blame. The tendency to fix blame is usually a fear-driven response on someone's part, and this often leads to lawsuits. Lawsuits and attorneys should be the last resort, not a way to fix blame.

Write it down

The simplest and most effective tool to avoid misunderstandings is to write things down! Resist the urge to think or act upon the idea of "Oh, I don't need to write it down with my good friend." WITSEC is the acronym for Federal Witness Security Program. My first WITSEC case, in one of my other careers, was a nice man from New Jersey. As mentioned before, I remember him telling me, "Stu, faded ink on the most yellowed paper is brighter than the clearest memory." His point, of course, was "Write it down!" If writing it down is good enough for organized crime, why wouldn't it be good enough for me?

Net Payment Versus Payment on Delivery

A criminal defense attorney I knew once told me this about fees. "What you don't get in advance, you don't get." In a winery context, always get deposits on custom orders, don't do in-house charge accounts, and only utilize major credit cards through national clearinghouses.

The exceptions to the "get it in advance rule" are wholesale accounts. Some wholesale accounts pay on receipt of goods, while others pay net thirty, which means in thirty days from receipt of goods. There is no single model for payment. It will depend upon your state laws and on locally accepted industry practice.

Keep a file on each wholesale customer. Track what they buy, who pays on time, and who is a slow payer. You can send goods to slow-paying accounts on a C.O.D. basis either through UPS or by common carrier. If timely payment is a continuing problem with a client, go to a pre-paid system with that account until the timely payment problem is resolved.

Have you heard of the three great truths? They are: "Never play cards with a man called Doc. Never eat at a place called Mom's. And never get into bed with anyone whose problems are worse than your own." Someone whose problems are worse than your own is difficult to assess sometimes, but rest assured the problems will be revealed.

Lawsuits and Why to Avoid Them

In a lawsuit, you will have to pay for your own attorney, and you may not be able to recover these up-front costs, even if you win. Before entering a lawsuit, see if your business insurance provides coverage. Try settlements and arbitration; and, having been there, I will tell you that the biggest obstacle to a settlement can be your ego. "Why settle when I was right and he was wrong? I was being victimized!"

Relative truth notwithstanding, "Which party is correct?" is, in fact, the wrong question to be asking. The better questions to be asking are, "How much can I afford to be right?" and, "How much is being judged right going to cost me and my business?" Once you start to think in terms of how much justice you can afford, you'll have made the essential leap to understanding that the cost of being right is at all times a business decision. I have settled lawsuits when I was clearly correct (in my mind) because I could not afford to be judged correct in a courtroom. There is a historic term for this concept: a "Pyrrhic victory," which is to say that winning too many expensive battles can cause you to lose the war.

Conclusions

Good planning and doing your business deals, offers, and contracts in writing are the way to do things. Always. Apply the same rules to friends as you would to strangers. Even at the risk of losing a short-term profit, disclose anything you know that the customer should know but apparently doesn't. All long-term business relationships are built on trust and reliability.

25.   Being a Consultant/Contractor

General business points:
- **IRS rules**

This chapter covers things I learned after being sued. If I am the sue-ee, then he was the sue-or. He claimed that I was his employee when I made wine from his raw material on a contract basis. I believed that I had always been an independent contractor. The case was settled through binding mediation, but only after both parties had helped their attorneys make multiple boat payments. Here is what I should have known going in.

Legal Definitions

What is the difference between being an independent contractor/consultant and being an employee? Your lawyer might explain that there are ten points the U.S. Supreme Court has cited in differentiating these two roles. Your accountant might also explain that there are twenty criteria the IRS uses to separate contractors from employees. The difference between contractors and employees does not just boil down to whether or not you are withholding payroll taxes from a person working for your business. Chief among the themes that the courts and IRS use are:

- Where is the work performed?
- Who sets the hours?
- Who specifies the tasks to be performed?
- Is there a contract involved?
- Is the work supervised?
- Is there a billing for services involved vs. an hourly or monthly wage?
- To whom does liability attach for work performed?
- Is there an employee performing the same work as the consultant?

Suffice it to say there were a lot more elements to this issue than I knew before I became a consultant. When in doubt, check with your accountant or the IRS.

Conclusions

Like it or not, the above tells you the standard upon which you will be judged by the IRS or the courts.

26. The Bar Call

General business points:
- **Intellectual property**
- **Compromise instead of lawsuits**

You've already read about my being sued over intellectual property, trademarks and formulas when I made wine on a contract basis. I'll repeat my expensive lesson about how much justice can you afford. The lawsuit only enriched several attorneys, but they have boat payments too, so I was helping keep our economy in motion.

Intellectual Property

When you're in business, you will become familiar with the concepts of trademarks and service marks. These concepts are the protection of words, names, or graphics to insure your exclusive use of the mark in a particular type of commerce, such as the wine business. Trademarks and service marks can be registered with the federal government and with the Secretary of State in each state. Registration is for a certain period of time and must be renewed periodically.

In my dealings with the local university that resulted in the creating of a Ewe Eye White parody label, I learned about the "common-law" trademark. University counsel informed me that besides specific images and names being exclusivized by registration, the totality of all registered trade and service marks, viewed collectively, constituted a "common-law" trademark. As a non-attorney, my takeaway from this was that a common-law trademark was something akin to the nature of the bar call, which I'll call the 'public's recognition' of, in this case, the university.

In the wine business, there is also the "bar call," which is the spoken sound of your brand name. Bar calls cannot be registered like trademarks and service marks but they do attach to registrations.

Some years ago, I received a phone call from the owner of Caymus Vineyards in Rutherford, CA. Because my winery (Camas) was listed alphabetically among the medal winners at the Los Angeles County Fair Wines of the World competition, I came to his attention. He explained the bar call concept to me and gave a clear example that I'll share with you. Suppose a customer in a wine bar should ask for a glass of Camas Chardonnay. Could the spoken sound of the winery name be confusing to the bartender so that he might mistake the request being for Caymus or vice versa? Simply put, does our winery name sound similar enough, to that of another winery to be confusing to customers or servers? I thanked the owner for this information.

Being Reasonable over Trying to Be "Right"

Several weeks later I received a business letter from the Caymus legal team asking us to change our winery name. Having consulted with my own liquor law specialist, I knew that a trial to determine if my winery name was too similar to the Caymus would be horribly expensive. My attorney described such a trial as being akin to a contest to see who is better at pitching gold doubloons off a bridge; even if you win, you lose! We responded and negotiated a settlement whereby we stopped using the name Camas.

We submitted to Caymus a list of suggested names: Camas Bloom, Camas Prairie, and Camas Flower, any of which would solve the bar call issue. They had no problem with any of these suggested alternatives. I settled on adopting the trade name of Camas Prairie for new labels. Since the bar call only concerns the spoken sound of the winery name, our graphics depicting a camas flower were never in question and did not need to change. Keeping this graphic minimized the effect of the name change on brand recognition. Everyone was happy, and it didn't cost me an arm and a leg in legal fees.

As it turned out, this potential bar call lawsuit benefited me in a way I hadn't expected. A winery can adopt and add to its basic permit any number of trade names, all of which then become legal for use on their labels. Trade names, once approved by the TTB, do not require new label approvals so the name change from Camas Winery to Camas Prairie Winery did not require new approvals for the labels previously approved under the Camas name. With the agreement in place and all my old paper labels about to be discarded, I found this was an opportunity to change over from paste-on labels to (new at the time) self-adhesive labels. Since I was eventually getting new labels anyway, my only extra expense was a new labeling machine. We turned a potential dispute into an opportunity to update and improve our packaging system. Now that's a settlement I can live with!

Being on the "Other End" of the Bar Call Issue

Ironically, in the ensuing years I twice found myself on the other end of a trademark or bar call issue. The first instance involved another Idaho winery that had released a wine with a label that included the name Sarah. I had registered a "Sarah's Blush" label a decade earlier. The second incident involved an Oregon winery that included "Camas" in their trade name.

I chose to pursue the first case involving "Sarah's Blush" because of the proximity between my winery and the other producer. I invested about $3,000 in legal fees to get this rival label removed from the distribution chain. As a courtesy, I allowed the other winery to sell off its existing labeled stock. The primary annoyance of this episode, other than my outlay of $3,000, was having this young winery owner fail to comprehend why I defended my intellectual property. Her position essentially was, "You shouldn't take all this so seriously. Wine should be fun."

The circumstance involving the Oregon winery with the "Camas" name was less expensive but not resolved in a satisfactory manner. I did not pursue the matter beyond an initial letter from my attorney, which merely requested them to make a name change. The winery declined; imagine that! I determined that their size and distance from my market made it unwise to devote more resources to press the issue. Not all battles need to be fought.

Conclusions

I didn't learn fast, but I learned good. Avoid lawsuits if at all possible and especially if mediation is a better financial decision. Find a friend in your own industry and ask about any peculiar rules that pertain to your product, like the bar-call in my case.

27. Mobile Bottling Services vs. Doing-it-Yourself

General business points:
- **Packaging options**
- **Purchase vs. rent**

When I started my winery in 1983 there was no such thing as a mobile bottling service. Nowadays, mobile bottling lines seem to be all the rage. These services pull up to your winery with a tractor-trailer and proceed to filter, bottle into sparged bottles (gassed with nitrogen to avoid oxygen transfer to the wine), cork, foil, and label your wines for an average cost of $2.50 per case. The $2.50 per case charge is for their services and not any of the components that you must have on hand. This service must be booked in advance, and there is usually an up-front deposit of several hundred dollars.

Back in 1983, I had to equip my winery to perform each of these operations. Nowadays, to equip a winery with comparable equipment—filler, corker, filter, foiler, labeler, and bottling tank—would cost a minimum of $25,000. Because I had already stocked my winery with this equipment, there was no economic incentive to abandon my in-house bottling operation when mobile bottling became available. However, believing as I do that life is a bunch of tradeoffs, I'll list some of the tradeoffs I see in using mobile bottling lines.

The Good about Hiring a Mobile Bottling Line

Using a mobile bottling line service will save you the initial expense of buying equipment to filter, bottle, cork, foil, and label your wines. You will save on the space for performing these same tasks (balance of space, remember?). You will save on supplies such as filter pads and industrial gasses which will be provided by the bottler.

The Neutral

You will still need to buy the same number of corks, foils, labels and bottles, but now you will have to buy them all at once to have on hand when the trailer shows up. You still need the same amount of floor space for dry storage of empty glass. You need more space because you may be bottling more wines at one time since the mobile bottler has limited scheduling dates available. You need to move pallet loads of both empty and full glass bottles to and from the bottling trailer.

The Unanticipated

You must have parking space at your winery for the bottling trailer. You must have exterior water and power available. You will struggle to get a reserved date for the trailer to arrive. All of your friends will need to help you out for at least one very long day. You will need to feed empty bottles to a dumping table and load full bottles back into cases at the other end of the filler line. The economics of mobile bottling may force you to bottle larger batches of wines at one time instead of smaller amounts in several batches. The minimum charge for the trailer is enough that overall bottling costs will rise significantly if you perform your bottling in several smaller batches. The economics of mobile bottling may force you to bottle some wines before or after their optimal bottling date.

The Unknown

There is a fixed cost to buying equipment. There will be maintenance costs, but basically once you own the equipment the use of it is free. If you bottle 2,500 cases annually at the $2.50 per case mobile bottling rate, in five years you will have spent $26,500 on mobile bottling services. Beyond five years, the economic advantages of using mobile bottling services vs. purchasing your own equipment largely disappear. However, the convenience factor of a mobile bottling service, and perhaps some special savings, would remain. Think of mobile bottling charges as rent. Just as with houses, at some point it is cheaper to buy than to continue renting. You have to do the math for your own circumstances. Remember my concept of balance in time, space, and money. Even if you can buy your own equipment, you must have the dedicated space to perform the operations that you would otherwise hire out.

Conclusions

As the chapter presented, there is no clear answer, industry to industry, as to the economic value of jobbing out any steps in your production process. Just know that the best answer for you may not be the obvious answer. Long term versus short term, start-up versus mature business, will also have different considerations. Here again, this is a time-space-money question. You need all three elements in balance to find the right way for your business.

28. Custom Crush, Bulk Wines and Virtual Wineries

General business points:
- ### Licensing options and strategies

This chapter is principally about the wine business and its evolution. I'll bet that evolution is endemic to most types of business.

Today there are licensing options that did not exist in 1983 when I became Idaho Bonded Winery #14. Back then I had to do it all, from crushing through bottling and labeling. The Bonded Winery license still exists as a popular option. Many new bonded wineries will utilize providers such as mobile bottling services to perform some of the aspects of turning grapes into bottled wine. Here are some new licensing options that make it easier to get into the business.

Shared Premises Operations

A shared premises permit allows multiple producers to share production space, with certain limits. The basic principal is that Winery A used the production equipment: crusher—press—filter—bottling line—labeling equipment, on a preset schedule. Winery B then uses the same equipment on different preset days. Each participating winery must keep their bulk wines in tanks marked as their own. Bottled wines for each winery must be stored separately and the same is true for separate and defined bonded wine storage areas.

A shared premises operation can perform wine-related services for customer wineries on a contract basis. There will be a menu of services: crushing, fermenting, aging, bottling, and labeling. You buy what service(s) you want and they are performed on a contract basis by and at the shared premises facility by one of its member wineries. Typically there will be a consulting enologist available to assist you, if you wish, perhaps at an extra charge.

When custom-crush facilities and options are viewed in conjunction with mobile bottling services, then we are approaching the new entity known as the virtual winery. The virtual winery concept is not a licensing option but it does open up licensing choices that didn't exist years ago.

Tax Paid Wine Bottling House

The second new licensing option is to be a "Tax Paid Wine Bottling House." In this licensing format you are buying finished wines that you resell. A Tax Paid Wine Bottling house licensee may be having bulk wine or unlabeled bottled wines delivered to them, or to a shared premises operation for bottling and labeling. In both cases, they use a licensed producer who sells services: crushing—fermenting—cellaring—blending—bottling—labeling.

The Virtual Winery

A virtual winery is a winery licensed by the TTB at a specific physical location, but many tasks involved in turning grapes into wines are being performed by hired hands off premises. The virtual winery might be characterized as having only paper equipment—licenses, money, and labels. Virtual wineries would use the label designation of "Cellared or Selected" instead of "Made, Produced or Vinted."

As someone who started a brick-and-mortar winery, I can see the appeal of a virtual winery. I now suffer from golfer's elbows, a bad knee, a tender lower back, and impinged shoulders.

Accepted by the Public?

To see how common these practices actually are, go to your local supermarket and pick a display shelf in the wine section. Check the backs of various bottles to see how many bottles on the shelf are labeled as "produced" or "made." Then count the number of bottles on the same shelf that read "cellared," "vinted," "selected," or "bottled for." The first group will be wines that were made by the labeled winery. The second group indicates the winery purchased wine made by someone else.

Are these virtual wineries wrong? Are they bad? Is this cheating? The answer is NO to all of these questions. But if you are transitioning from a virtual winery, it would be wise not to move into a hybrid or brick-and-mortar operation until you have solved the Gordian knot of selling your wine.

Conclusions

My introductory paragraph said it all; the rules change. Stay on top of the changes. Some are advantageous and others not. Read the trade journals for your industry. Is there a trade group you can join? Do so. While you have your time filled with the day-to-day operation of your business, the law and the industry move on. After the 9-11 attacks, our banking rules changed, and so did our product production records requirements. We now had to track the origin of our raw materials for any food item. Don't get left behind.

29. Selling to Retail Customers

General business points:
- **Retail sales skills**
- **Customer service**

There are many books discussing the topic of selling at the retail level. What follows is my best advice based on my personal sales experience. I make no claims beyond sharing what worked for me.

Welcoming the Customer

First, greet all customers within thirty seconds of their entering the store. Pick your own phrase. I chose, "Welcome to the winery. How can I help you?" If I was working alone in the tasting room with a customer when another customer entered the store, I'd still perform the greeting within thirty seconds. I'd find a natural pause in the interaction with my current customer, then say, "Excuse me, one second," and proceed to give my greeting to the new arrival. I did not stop dealing with my original customer, I just acknowledged the new arrival and added, "Have a look around, and I'll be with you in just a bit." I neither ignored the new customer nor left the customer with whom I was already involved. I think that people come to a winery for the experience as much as for the actual wine. Make sure their experience is a good one.

Product Knowledge is to Help, Not Show off

As the years wore on, I naturally acquired a ton of product knowledge, having been in the business as winemaker, grower, and owner for more than three decades. But I was careful not to try and impress customers with my knowledge. I wanted to use my knowledge in such a way that it would help the customer, rather than appear as if I was showing off. Presenting knowledge without pretentiousness worked best for me as I tried to give

111

information in a way that would resonate with something the customer already knew.

For example, the tasting sequence affects our experience and enjoyment of wine. While describing the tasting experience to a customer, I might use the following dialogue. "Think of how the first swig of orange juice tastes after you've brushed your teeth. The orange juice didn't magically start tasting bad, but the sequence of coming after toothpaste made the first few sips taste bad."

When discussing whether white wines should be served chilled, I might say something like "Sometime in your life, you had a sip of a warm Coke. The same Coke that is crisp and just sweet enough when cold is thick and syrupy when warm. So, you see, chilling minimizes our perception of sugars and makes things crisper." These are examples of how you can use a customer's own experience to give your teaching instant credibility. No matter how knowledgeable you are, you're viewed as unbelievable if your audience does not validate your message in their own minds.

Becoming an Expert in the Customer's Mind

Getting the customer to accept you as an expert means understanding that what you are selling is not just a product. You are selling product, service, and confidence. The product is your wine. The service is you going out of your way to make sure the customer is as happy with their purchase at home as they were in your store. Put product and service together and you create confidence for the customer. The customer is confident in their choice and confident you did your best to help them get what they wanted. Confidence builds long-term relationships between customers and stores. Be the person that helps the customer look like an expert to their guests.

Remember that selling is about the customer. Think of how much money you may have spent on advertising. If you paid to get them in your tasting room, you don't want to waste what might be your only chance to keep them there. The magic word in selling is YOU, and don't forget that.

- "How can I help You?"
- "Is there something that You would like to try?"
- "Would You like to have a cold bottle of the wine You picked so it will be ready to serve?"

then most importantly,

- "What else can I do for You?"

and finally,

- "Thank You for coming in. I appreciate Your business."

Selling is Different from Clerking

Selling is engaging and interacting with customers in a mutually beneficial way. Selling is not about being pushy, but is instead about being brave enough to enhance the sales relationship after the initial purchase.

"Welcome to the winery. How can I help you today?"

Answer: "I'm just looking." If you as the greeter stop there, you are clerking, not selling. Selling begins when the customer is not actively buying.

Rather than stopping your interaction when you hear "Just looking," try some version of, "Great! Welcome. Have you been in before?"

The customer must now respond and interact with you. He may say, "I've been in before," or, "No, this is my first time."

Continue to interact by responding with "Welcome back; let me know if you see anything you'd like to try" or "OK, great. Let me quickly show you what you walked into, to make your browsing easier." Another great starter question to use with customers is, "Are you looking for something for dinner or something for the cellar?"

In my tasting room, I quickly described how the wines and beers were displayed. My wines were arranged from dry to sweet with information cards at each wine that showed price, vintage, and residual sugar. The beer display contained brews sorted by color, and descriptions of each beer were posted on the corresponding shelf in the beer case. Finally, I mentioned that all the wines and all the beers were available by the glass in our non-smoking wine bar. I then moved off with a parting shot, "So, let me know if you see something you'd like to taste or have any questions." The keys here are that I was brief, informative, and a resource for the customer. I did not hover. And I always left with a smile.

Suggestion Selling

Selling continues the entire time the customer is in your store, so I developed my approach to suggestion selling. The customer says, "I'd like a bottle of Merlot." A simple clerk would stop there, ring up the purchase and be done. A suggestion seller would set the bottle of Merlot on the counter and then do one or more of the following things as best fit the circumstance. "How many folks are you serving?" or "Are you sure that one bottle will be enough?" Be careful to not put customers on the defensive here. Do some quick mental math if the sale is for a meal. If you know the group size, say six wine drinkers, then one bottle will not yield six servings. This may be something that the customer hadn't considered. You can also try; "What else can I get for you?" or "Did you see anything _____?" and filling in the blank with words such as: "anything else," "anything you're curious about," "anything new since your last visit that you'd like to taste." This is called the UP-SELL!

Up-Selling

If the customer purchased two or three bottles, I might say something about our case discounts. "Most wineries start their discounts when you buy a case, but we give you a discount on any six bottles. So, if you got only a few more bottles now, you would get a nice discount on your entire purchase." The same goes for talking the customer up to a case of twelve. "Wow, three more bottles and all your wine is 10 percent off." I also bumped my discount up on a three-case purchase from ten to fifteen percent per case. Here, my pitch was: "Okay, you've got two cases of fine wines. If you consider getting one more case we'll raise the discount to fifteen percent on all your wine."

In casual conversation with the customer, if I learned that some of the wine being purchased was a gift, I would ask, "Do you need gift bags for any of these?" Another suggestion sale opportunity! I kept selling until the customer told me they were done. But be careful to never decide for yourself, through words or actions, that the customer is done.

Customer Service as Part of the Sale

Once the customer was finished with their selections, I switched to customer-service actions to help build or expand relationships. For example, the purchase includes some white wines, so I'd ask, "Can I get you chilled bottles of any of your wines so they are ready to serve?" or "Would it be better for you if I put your wines in a free cardboard box or is a bag better?"

Preferred Customer Cards

We had a preferred customer card program, which is like a latté punch card—buy one, get a punch. Just like all punch card programs, you get something of value. In our system, the customer scored an additional discount when the card was filled. I asked every customer, "Do you have one of our preferred customer cards?" If they did not, I started a new card for them. If they had a card already, I gave them a punch for each bottle of their current purchase.

Maybe you have a wine club program that would appeal to an out-of-town customer. Maybe the out-of-town customer is flying home and could take wine home with them as checked baggage if they only knew you had shipper boxes and that taking wine as checked baggage was permitted. Or, maybe a customer traveling on vacation would be more apt to buy if they knew that you were a UPS, FedEx, or DHL shipping station. In each of these cases, the customer must know about the services you offer for both of you to benefit.

When You Don't Have What the Customer Wants

Sometimes customers asked for products that I did not make or sell. They might have confused my tasting room with a wine shop, or maybe they were looking for hard liquor. No problem. I would gladly direct them to a local store that offered what they needed. Sometimes I used this as another opportunity to sell. If a customer came in looking for a varietal that I didn't produce, I would tell them where they could get what they wanted, but also tell them about what I had that was similar and emphasize that they could try my wines before purchase.

For example, a customer is looking for Zinfandel, which I don't make. I would reply, "I don't have a Zinfandel because it's not grown in this region and I only make wine from good local fruit. I do have a Merlot that you might like. Would you like a free taste of the Merlot?" Once I got them to taste wines, I could steer them from the Merlot to Cabernet or another product. I emphasized, "This isn't Zinfandel, but it's very similar and you'll know exactly what you'll be getting."

All of these examples are services to the customer that are non-profit for the business, but they establish in the mind of the customer a connection through service. This is what repeat business is all about. Service builds loyalty and confidence, so the customer views you as a resource, a consultant, an expert, and a friend. Approach the concept of selling like dating. If you never ask, you never get a "Yes."

Conclusions

Everything we make must at some time be sold and perhaps resold after that. Selling is about meeting the customer's needs. Be knowledgeable about your product and industry but apply the knowledge in the service of the customer and not your own ego.

30.   Spacing Out Work Over the Year

General business points:
- **Time management**

Working full-time as I did made it difficult to free up time for crushing grapes. To deal with this time crunch issue, I began making wines from products other than grapes. This strategy allowed me to space out my winemaking to more months of the year. I made honey-based wine, which is also called mead, and later added honey/berry combinations and wild plum wine.

Honey is available almost year-round, so I could make a batch of mead on an as-needed basis. The same was true for the honey and berry combination wines if I used commercially raised and sourced frozen berries. Wild plums ripened in late July, which allowed me to make this wine before the grape harvest. Not only did this strategy of making non-grape wines in addition to a number of classic grape varieties space out my work, but it allowed me to get more total production out of a physically smaller facility. I was using the same tanks and product area several times a year instead of producing only grape wines and using the product area once a year.

An example of spacing out production

Making 5,000 gallons of grape wine would require tankage and fermenters for 5,000 gallons at one time. Making 5,000 total gallons of wine that was 2,000 gallons of honey-based wines, 500 gallons of fruit wine, and 2,500 gallons of grape wines only took about 3,000 gallons of tankage and fermenters.

Here's how.

- Make the mead any time before July 15, and it's ready to be bottled by September 1. That allows all the tankage and fermenters to be available for grape crush.

117

- Make plum wine in July or August and it is ready to bottle by Sept. 15, so again no loss of production capacity or space for the grape crush.

I further increased available time by adding sparkling wines to my product line. Sparkling wines are twice-fermented wines. The secondary fermentation takes place in the bottle for traditional Champagne-style sparkling wines. I would make the base wine for my sparklers in the fall. The base wine, called cuvée, would be ready for secondary fermentation around February. Once the secondary fermentation was complete, I could finish (riddle, disgorge and dosage) small amounts of sparkling wine at a time of my choosing.

These options and approaches allowed me to maximize my winemaking season and minimize the extent to which my day job and my winery job clashed.

Conclusions

If possible in your particular business, arrange production to maximize your available time. Can you make some non-perishable components in advance of need? If yours is a food or beverage business, can you adapt products to use less perishable materials? Engineer your business to have as few time-crunch situations as possible.

31.   Selling and Service to Wholesale Customers

General business points:

- **Customer support**

As mentioned in previous chapters, rules and regulations for alcoholic beverages vary greatly from state to state. The services a winery can provide for its customers are no exception. What is perfectly legal in one state might be unlawful in another. My comments in this chapter are therefore very general in nature and should be checked against your own state's laws.

Support Services You Can Provide the Customer

Whenever a restaurant in my local area chose to offer a selection of my wines, I would provide free "wine service" training to the restaurant staff. This showed the restaurant owner that I saw their financial success as important to me. The restaurant staff may have very little experience in the proper techniques for opening wine, serving wine, providing wine sampling, recommending wines, and getting the customer's approval of a bottle of wine. Your knowledge in these areas is an asset to your customer, so make sure you view your knowledge as something to share.

A good suggestion to make to your restaurant customers is to allow their servers of legal age to sample the wines on the restaurant's wine list. This imparts to the staff a certain amount of product knowledge and increases their comfort with the wine list. In the case of wines that are not sampled by the servers, you can demonstrate how to understand a wine label.

A restaurant's staff can also be taught to make wine recommendations based on their own honest preferences and knowledge. However, I greatly discourage teaching anyone to fake knowledge of wines. I refer to this as the "When Harry Met

Sally" system. Don't try faking it like Sally did! It's better to admit your limitations and say something along the lines of, "I'm not sure. Let me ask our (chef, owner, wine director) and come right back." This is a better strategy for the staff, as it stresses honesty and lets them know it's OK with the boss for them to ask questions.

Training Services Available for Your Customer's Staff

How many times have you seen a waiter struggle to open a bottle of wine? Show the staff the correct way to use a corkscrew and the best corkscrews to use. And make sure you offer those corkscrews for sale! I've found the best method for teaching wine opening techniques is to make up a few dummy wine bottles filled with water. I then let my students practice on those bottles. Encourage your students to choose the corkscrew they are the most comfortable with.

Some servers, for a variety of reasons, may be intimidated by the wine list. If so, you need to raise their comfort level with wines in general—primarily so they won't default to suggesting beer to the diner. Over the years, I developed a method for raising the comfort level of novice wait staff where wine is concerned. I call it the Stu System. Under the Stu System, the novice server can recommend a wine after asking two simple questions:

(1) "Do you prefer a dry wine or one with a hint of sweetness?"
(2) "Would you prefer a red wine or maybe something lighter?"

With the answers to these two questions and familiarity with as few as four wines on their wine list, the novice server has a workable base of information from which to serve customers until his or her wine knowledge has expanded. Of course, for the Stu System to work, the server must have tried at least four wines from the restaurant's wine list. These four wines should represent the four basic wine types on the wine list—dry red, dry white, off dry white, and either blush or rosé.

The answer to the first question—dry or not dry—allows the server to eliminate part of the wine list. The server should understand the meaning of dry in 'wine speak', in case the diner has questions. The second question—red or not red—allows the server to eliminate half of the remaining list, leaving the server with a single wine to recommend.

All of this training will increase the servers' confidence in their ability to sell and serve wines. They may be more inclined to recommend one of your wines because they'll see you as someone who was helpful to them. As an added bonus, the staff will discover that the sale of a bottle of wine is the equivalent of selling another entrée, which in turn increases their tip. Everyone—the winery, the restaurant owner, and the servers—will benefit from your knowledge and training.

Always remember that your wholesale customers are your friends, and always buy from your friends because your enemies aren't buying from you. Some things are more obvious than others and this is one of those things. Patronize the restaurants and stores that sell your wines. Say hello to the owner/chef/grocery manager every time you see them. Your presence lets them know that you value their business. If possible, talk to your wholesale customers when you visit them. Do they have anything coming up that you can help them with? Your offer of help will be remembered and appreciated.

Above all, don't be all talk and no action. Keep waiter's wine keys (cork screws) in stock so restaurant staff will come to you for their supplies. Know the rules in your state(s) as to the legal assists you can give your customers. For example, teaching table service to new staff may be legal but giving anything of value—such as glasses, cork screws, or printed wine lists—may not be legal.

Know the rules about in-store tastings. Is a catering permit required? Are there limits on sampling wine such as the maximum number of tastes allowed or the required use of a closed or defined area—the proverbial velvet rope—for the tasting? If you are performing an in-store tasting, remember to verify a person's age before serving them samples. If you or your distributor serves an underage person, it's your customer who is penalized—and possibly the pourer.

Check up on Your Distributor's Service to the Customer

Is your distributor giving your patrons the service they deserve? Does the distributor call on them regularly? Do they participate in resets as needed? Are they filling the orders properly, on time, and not over stocking the customer? If you don't ask, you might not know until your wines disappear from the wine list or store shelf. Never forget that every contact with a customer is an opportunity to sell! And remember the magic word in selling is—You! "What can I do for You?" sells both your product and your service.

Your Wholesale Customer Base

Never stop trying to open new retail customers! I discovered that whenever I thought my list of retail accounts had stabilized, something negative happened. The events that disrupted my peace and joy included accounts that changed hands, closed, or changed their wine list. I needed to constantly open new accounts just to maintain a certain level of wholesale volume. If a store or restaurant closed, their business was lost forever. If the same store or restaurant changed hands, I usually had to compete for the new owner's business. If the new owner already had a similar business elsewhere, they might want to use their current set of suppliers. Be prepared for issues such as these.

Restaurants sometimes respond to customer demands for the "new darling" in wines. Yesterday, Chardonnay was hot; today it's not. Because wine is trendy and market research shows that five percent of the buying public buys ninety percent of the wine, sometime(s) you will be caught behind the trend. You may not have "today's darling" (be it Marsanne or Malbec) that has the consumers buzzing, which can cost you a spot on the wine list. The "today's darling" phenomenon can be minimized by good selling practices in your tasting room, but in the mind of a restaurateur, who always wants what his customers are asking for, you may have a problem.

Homework before Approaching a Potential Customer

In my attempts to open new retail accounts, I always checked back with potential customers who originally said "no" to my approaches. I tracked which accounts could potentially move from the "no" column to the "yes" column. With the potential "yes" folks, I calendared follow-up contacts—perhaps in four, six, or twelve months. In the follow-up visit, I'd prepare myself with knowledge of the customer's business by walking the store or, in restaurants, reviewing the menu and wine lists. Before approaching a decision maker, always arm yourself with as much knowledge as possible.

When calling on restaurants, I would offer specific suggestions about which of my wines would fill a gap in their wine list. I was prepared to tell them the per-ounce cost of my wines to show price worthiness in a by-the-glass wine program. I would ask how they priced their wines—such as a 200% mark-up on cost, plus $2)—and then show them the price points of my wines on their wine list. Knowing and being able to show the price worthiness of my wines made sense to restaurateurs and often got me on their wine list.

When dealing with stores, I used a variety of suggestions to generate interest in my wines. I might present a particularly apropos item, such as my sweet dessert red wine, to accompany chocolates around Valentine's Day. I might suggest a wine with a regional connection, such as Huckleberry—the state berry of Idaho—in tourist towns. The regional connection might be my custom Cougar Label series for stores that sold near Washington State University. Or, the local connection might be using fruit from a particular vineyard that was near my potential customer's locations.

I never stopped looking for new accounts because there is a normal lifecycle to businesses; they start up, grow, mature, and finally die. Some businesses die by failing. Others die by being sold. Still others die by changing their identity. The customers you have today are not guaranteed to be there tomorrow. Keep in mind that you are constantly building and maintaining your business to enhance its salability in the future. So, never stop selling.

The Stall

When a customer can't say no and is afraid to say yes.

I also learned to recognize the stall. Some customers would rather tell you to see them in four months than tell you they are just not interested. When asked to call back in a specific period of time, I honored that request. If I was put off again, then I wrote off that account unless, or until, it changed ownership or management. Then I tried again.

Ideas about Who Might Be a New Customer

I learned the value of listening to tasting room customers when they talked about a newly discovered restaurant. I showed interest when customers told me about wine outlets where they wished to find my wines. If their comments pointed me to an unfamiliar account, I'd request more information from my customer. Where was the outlet? Who was the manager or owner? Could I mention their name when I called on the outlet? In this manner I received good leads on new potential accounts and my customers appreciated my following up on their suggestions.

Conclusions

Think about all the time and money you've spent advertising to get customers. When approaching a potential customer, do some homework in advance so you appear knowledgeable about their needs. Satisfied customers will be a source of referrals for future potential customers. Businesses have a lifespan, so today's customers may retire or otherwise be gone tomorrow, so never stop looking for future customers. Recognize the value of your existing customers and support them in every way possible. Can you help their staff be more comfortable and competent in dealing with your product(s)? Never forget, if they don't make money, you don't make money!

Bottom line; constantly seek new accounts to make up for accounts you lose through the normal life cycles of business. I've just one caution to accompany my thoughts about always trying to open new accounts: Know your production capacity and your ability to supply wine reliably to customers. Don't seek business that you cannot reasonably supply. Seek balance between your production and your sales.

32. Consumer Education, Wine 101

General business points:
- **Selling consumer education as a product**

I began teaching a consumer education class called "Wine 101." I've always believed that the wine industry made a strategic mistake in the 1960s when they tried to create an image of wine as more sophisticated than beer. The net effect of this approach was that young people were scared of wine. The wine terminology and rules of proper wine usage were daunting to these people, so they avoided wine altogether.

Whenever possible, I used a consumer's prior life experiences to enlighten them about wine, like orange juice after toothpaste or warm Coke vs. cold Coke. I taught only enough nomenclature to be helpful. A customer need only know the meaning of a few basic terms—dry, tart, tannic, bouquet—to accurately communicate their desires. They do not need to know everything I know about wine nor do they need an in-depth knowledge of the terminology on the University of California-Davis twenty-point scale. I emphasized that questions are good and made attendees more comfortable with ordering-choosing-serving wine.

The Keys to Teaching

For my "Wine 101" class, I used a technique that the U.S. Army drilled into me: Tell the audience what you intend to tell them, tell them, and finally tell them what you told them. I started by explaining and showing (making a faux glass of wine using water, alcohol, pigment, sugar, salts and acid) what is in wine. I explained how our physical senses worked. I explained how wine should be tasted. The swirling, sniffing, sipping mechanics of proper wine tasting make sense once you understand how our physical senses operate and interact. Only then do the mechanics of wine tasting became more than mere rituals to the consumer.

Learning theory holds that each time you add an additional sense to the learning process for a single bit of information you double the retention rate for that information. So, if I told my class attendees something (sense of hearing) and also let them taste an example (sense of taste), I doubled the chance they would understand and retain that information.

I also used simple but uncommon methods to increase understanding and retention of information. For example, I showed that certain components of taste are experienced in different areas of the mouth. The students learned not only 'how' something tasted but also 'where' in their mouth it was tasted. This was valuable in teaching the difference between tart and tannic, as these taste components of wine are often confused and misunderstood. Similarly, the difference in perceived sweetness from sugar vs. alcohol can be taught more easily by linking the experiences to their physical location in the mouth.

Conclusions

Product and service should go together at both wholesale and retail levels. Do what you can to increase your customers' comfort level with your product(s). Teaching is about the customers and their needs, not about you showing off. Try to teach competence from the basis of what they already know. Repetition is essential to retention of information. Hands-on experiences teach better than telling or showing alone. Knowledge and experience can be adapted, sometimes more easily than acquired.

33. Catering Services

General business points:

- **A product/service sales combination**

Think about service as a product unto itself. Sell it. Can you sell your clothing line at house parties where you do a mini-fashion show? Co-promote your salsa or cheese at in-store tastings where you sample and sell? Service is an almost unlimited expander of product sales opportunities.

Catering

Catering can open a tremendous sales market for a winery, especially if the winery offers complete catering services including servers, glasses, coolers, and ice buckets. Catering sales can also be significantly increased by adding beer and sparkling wine to your offerings. The magic word here is service. By partaking of your catering services, your customer saves himself a hassle at every level of beverage service: from arranging glass rentals to figuring out how to chill or transport large quantities of beer and wine. But the benefit your customer receives from your catering service does not end there.

Make your expertise available

You can use your expertise to suggest appropriate wines for specific events and to impart knowledge of standard service ratios. Explain to your customers that service ratios refer to the standard size of a single serving of wine. They'll appreciate knowing that a standard wine pour is five ounces and a single 750 ml bottle will provide five pours. If the event calls for sparkling wines, explain that the service size is three ounces with eight servings per bottle. This knowledge can help your customer predict the minimum number of bottles he'll need to purchase for his event.

Number of choices

The average customer will not be aware that too many wine choices can complicate beverage service, but too few choices do not cover the major wine groups. Explain to your customer that having three styles of wine is a perfect variety for any event—a dry red, a dry white, and a slightly sweet white or blush. Within these three wine groups, it really doesn't matter if you have Merlot or Syrah, Chardonnay or Pinot Grigio. It just matters that the options of a dry white, dry red, and lightly sweet wine are offered.

Know the regulations

Catering services also include knowing the local regulations. This keeps you out of trouble and makes life easier for your customer. Do you need a catering permit from your city, county, or state? Do you need to be licensed in the state? What types of beverage choices can you cater with your particular license?

Remember, your experience allows you to make complex events simpler for your customers. Who needs more worries on their child's wedding day? Offering a catering service is selling peace of mind.

Conclusions

Play the service card to create sale opportunities. Do the same with a consumer education component to become the resident expert in your particular market. As mentioned in the introduction to this chapter, service in some form is both a product and a sales multiplier that can benefit your business.

34. Staffing from the Staff Perspective

General business points:
- **Income levels**
- **Training**
- **Policy/procedures manual**
- **Employee fidelity**
- **Industrial psychological issues**

The Employee's Financial Needs

Your staff members, like everyone else, have household budgets. They need to know their current income and their future income potential. Your staff's stability and mental comfort is enhanced if new employees receive a written statement of their salary or wage ladder. What do they make while they are being trained? Do they get a raise once they are trained? When might they be eligible for a raise, and how much of a raise will it be? What is the top salary they can reasonably expect to make? Are there other ways they can increase their earnings, such as through commission sales or working hours at outside events? Raises will, of course, be merit-based and you are not promising a raise. Rather, you are explaining what pay increases they are eligible to receive in the future.

Cutting Staff Hours

To further stabilize the staff's ability to plan their budgets, avoid the temptation to cut employee hours when things are slow. My winery had predictably slow times, usually in parallel with the class schedules of the two local colleges. When school is out—spring break, summer—things get slow in a college town. Additionally, the month of February was always a slow time because families had used their Christmas money and were now saving to pay taxes in April. My staff's rents, food costs, and car payments were not magically adjusted downward to suit my seasonal needs. I learned that keeping good employees meant being mindful of their financial stability, lest I suffer the cost and trouble of hiring and training a constant stream of new employees.

Emergency Loans

When I started hiring employees I put into place "The Bank of Stu" to make loans to staff members. The concept for The Bank of Stu grew out of my law enforcement experience. While serving in law enforcement, I saw a regular parade of bank embezzlers whose crimes could have been avoided with a simple loan program.

In my experience, the average embezzler was a young or middle-aged woman who discovered one Friday that she needed a small amount of money for groceries, gas, a drink after work with co-workers, or a birthday present for her kid. She happened to be broke this particular Friday, so she borrowed $20 from her cash drawer with plans to put it back unnoticed on the following Monday. You can probably guess the next part of the story. When Monday rolled around, she found she couldn't put the money back. She spent the entire week in mortal terror, fearing that her small criminal act would soon be discovered. But she was not discovered; after a while she stopped being scared and borrowed from the cash drawer again. As time went on and her debt grew, she finally gave up on paying back the money, and put out of her mind the consequences of her actions. When her actions were inevitably discovered, the scope of the theft had mushroomed and she was prosecuted.

I observed that these embezzlers were mostly folks who never dreamed of committing a robbery or an assault, but they each fell victim to human nature. I'm not saying that it is human nature to do bad things. I'm saying that we are all fallible human beings and sometimes we make bad choices. I further believe that if banks had a small emergency fund for their employees who needed $20 on Friday, many a criminal episode would be avoided.

So, back to the winery! If banks, with all their surveillance cameras, can't keep their employees from stealing, how likely was it that I could keep my staff from "borrowing" money under similar circumstances? My best idea was to help honest folk stay honest. The Bank of Stu was created to be the option that never existed for those poor bank employees. As part of their initial week of paid training, staff was told about The Bank of Stu, its purpose, and how they could access The Bank's funds. I explained that my telling them about The Bank did not reflect any concerns that I had about them, but was rather a recognition that "shit happens." Before they developed a long-term disaster out of a short-term problem, I wanted them to turn to The Bank of Stu.

Keep Training Simple and Practical

I found that my staff was much less anxious if there were fewer job details to memorize. Simplifying my systems made it easier for staff to acquire needed skills and less likely they would get confused and make mistakes. For example, each new staff member sampled all of my wines during training—I wanted them to know what they were selling. I told each new staff member that I expected them to have favorites among my wines, just as I had my own favorites. I told them to share with customers their own experiences and preferences. Instead of handing my staff a selling script to memorize, I taught them to be honest with customers and use their own words—good or neutral—to describe the wines. If they did not like a particular wine, I suggested they simply reply, if asked, "That is not my favorite style of wine, so I'll let you form your own opinion."

Procedures Manual

Having a Camas Prairie Training and Procedures manual in the tasting room reduced the amount of information employees had to memorize—if in doubt, they could look it up. As with all of us, things I do on a daily basis become routine for me. Then there are tasks that I perform infrequently, which are the tasks on which I am more likely to make a mistake. I found the best plan was to give each employee a week of paid training where they did nothing but observe me and the current staff as we dealt with customers, labeled bottles, packed shipments, and stocked the tasting room. After watching us for a while, the new hires then advanced to working on tasks with us, and finally to performing those same tasks on their own.

Your Location Can Affect Your Pay Schedule

Finally, an important note that may fit your own geographic circumstance. In 2019, Idaho still uses the Federal minimum wage—currently $7.25 per hour—while Washington State mandates a minimum wage of $12.50 per hour. To be fair to my employees and to minimize staff turnover, I paid my staff based on the current Washington minimum wage. It was not rocket science to foresee that I would lose employees from Moscow if they found a job eight miles away in Pullman, Washington for $5.25 more per hour. (When I sold in 2011 the wage differential was $1.92 per hour). I may have lost money in the short run but I believe I saved money in the long run through reducing the cost of hiring and training new employees.

What Industrial Psychology Can Teach Us

Through the years I always strove to keep my employees happy. Along with The Bank of Stu and my insistence on paying the Washington minimum wage in Idaho, I also applied some useful information I learned in college. When I was a psych grad student back in 1973, I took a course in Industrial Psychology. Many years ago, there was a study of human behavior done at the Hawthorne Gasworks. Employees were told that researchers were trying to confirm previous findings suggesting that changes to the work environment would make the employees more comfortable. One employee group was told that raising the office temperature one degree would improve their comfort level. Another group was told that lowering the office temperature by one degree would improve their comfort. Some were told their office lighting would be brightened while others were told their office lights would be slightly dimmed: all in the name of their comfort.

In truth, the researchers were testing how the employees' mindsets and beliefs—the boss is doing something to make my workspace nicer—would affect their job performance. In the various test areas, temperatures were not changed either up or down. The lighting of work areas was neither increased nor decreased. But in every case the employee groups showed improvement in productivity and expressed increased satisfaction with their jobs. The study concluded that people were happier and more productive if they believed their bosses cared about them and were trying to make their workplace better. Hawthorne showed the power of the mind in making us happy!

Job Satisfaction

The second thing I remember from that long-ago college course is Herzberg's Theory of Work. Herzberg's research concerned the factors that make a job satisfying. He concluded that job satisfaction is based on recognition, achievement, responsibility, and employee interest in the job. Money was not found to contribute to job satisfaction.

Herzberg concluded that what caused job dissatisfaction was not simply the opposite of what causes job satisfaction. He identified that negative perceptions of company policy, administration, supervision, and individual salary were all significant contributors to job dissatisfaction.

Specific to salary, too little money—feeling underpaid—was apt to make someone dissatisfied with his job. But belief by an employee that he was adequately paid or even well paid did not make up for the fact that he didn't enjoy his work.

Herzberg found that money is only a factor in job dissatisfaction. Throwing more money at employees can only raise their job satisfaction level from a negative point to neutral. More money will not move their satisfaction level from neutral to the positive.

As employers, we get improved results by adding job enrichment programs. In my business, I made employees feel valued by requesting their input on important matters. For example, we all tasted and then voted on beers that I was considering stocking—if my employees did not like a beer that I happened to like, I refused to offer that beer for sale. I also solicited input from my employees on wine blending options. I paid cash bonuses for employee ideas that I put into practice. I consulted them on label changes, promotional plans, and changes to product lines. A valued employee is a satisfied employee.

Conclusions

When business is slow, cutting your hours as a money saver will be at the expense of your employees' incomes and household budgets. Cutting their income to save your own is a tempting but bad short-term move. While we can only pay what we can afford, try to see things from an employee's point of view.

What is crystal clear to us may be totally new and confusing to a new hire. Place a value on training; keep it simple and clear. You will build an employee's self-confidence, value and willingness to stay on the job if you train them properly. Training is a cost saver when you consider the cost in time/money of the hiring process. Having a Policy and Procedures manual is essential both as a training aid and for setting out your expectations.

Unfortunately people steal. Sometimes they steal out of necessity: think Les Miserables. Sometimes they steal out of a sense of entitlement because they feel unappreciated and overworked. Having an employee emergency fund can help with both of the above situations. Depending on the volume of money at risk, you can also insure against loss through the purchase of an Employee Fidelity Bond: a type of insurance.

My two paragraphs about industrial psychology explain often unseen or unacknowledged truths about human behavior. Employees respond to being cared about by the boss. Money will never make someone like a job, and too little money will make them dislike a job. Recognition and self-satisfaction are key to keeping your people happy.

35. Staffing from the Owner's Perspective

General business points:

- **Recognizing your own limits and goals**

So now we are more attuned to the employee's perspective. We need to be brutally honest about our own issues. My own issues hinged on finding out that there were aspects of self-employment that I hadn't thought about until there was an unavoidable clash. I didn't like having to hire people. The interviewing, selection and training weren't what I wanted to do. Neither were doing the books, figuring overhead, being a janitor or collecting from overdue accounts, but they were part of the deal.

As your experiences with your business will soon reveal, there are plenty of varied and complex issues that come with being an employer. I hope some of the lessons I've learned will help you out.

First of all, the boss needs to know more than the staff! You have to know the entire system because in a small winery operation, you are the trainer. Tasting room jobs are not careers, so there will be a regular staff turnover. Maybe you are situated in a college town as I was, where the turnover rate is increased by staff members who graduate and move away. In a winery, the trainer holds a key position.

Retired folks make excellent tasting room employees because they may only want limited hours and already have some retirement income. Employee discounts are also very attractive to retirees.

Another reason to know more than your staff is to decrease the chances of theft. The likelihood of theft by employees is greater if you omit systems that monitor what goes out and what comes in. Think of this like President Reagan's statement about doing business with the Soviet Union: "Trust but verify." Also, keep your employees clear on what is acceptable behavior and what is not. I had a form that spelled out the ten deadly sins that would be grounds for termination:

1. Theft of goods or money
2. Theft by giving free drinks or unauthorized discounts to friends
3. Not showing up for work
4. Failing to properly card for proof of age
5. Being in the shop after hours without permission
6. Mislabeling of wine by variety or vintage—second offense
7. Leaving doors unlocked at closing
8. Inaccurate entries in Removed Tax Paid inventory book—second offense
9. Incorrect pricing or discounting on any wine sale—third offense
10. Lying about compliance with any of the deadly sins.

And finally, you must know everything about the operating systems of the business so you can track what is working procedurally and what is not working. Inefficiency costs money!

Being Honest and Self-Aware

During my career in law enforcement, I once received training for mediating crises and resolving hostage situations. My training did not involve weapons or tactics, but rather techniques to verbally defuse situations before utilizing measures of last resort. The main thrust of the training was to get the subject talking. The subject might be a suicidal person, a barricaded person, or a hostage-taker, but in each case the approach was the same. The technique consisted of establishing dialogue by asking three questions: What do you want? How are you going to get it? Is what you're doing working? So, as the business owner, what do you want? How are you going to get it? Is what you're doing working?

To answer these questions you need a vision, a plan, a method of analyzing your performance, and a set of performance measures. Once your vision, or business model, is clear, you can determine the number of staff you will need. I can't give you a magic number for staffing because the twin evils of short-staffing and over-staffing are specific to your business plan and circumstance. I can, however, offer a list of questions that will serve as a guide. Some of your answers to these questions may change as you learn more about yourself, your labor market, and your customers, so don't be forever wedded to your previous decisions. Never feel guilty about "going back to school" to learn new things regardless of how many diplomas and licenses you've previously earned.

On to the Questions:

Owner Involvement?

Are you, your spouse, or your children going to work in the business? If so, what jobs will each of you perform? How many hours will each of you work? What could go wrong, such as other obligations, transportation issues, school time, or parenting demands? Be realistic and honest.

Life Outside Business?

Do you plan to take vacations? Who will provide coverage if you are gone? How much time can you devote comfortably to the business on a daily basis? Be sure to factor in commute time.

Operating Hours?

What operating hours will you advertise for the tasting room? Will these hours require two shifts of employees in order to avoid paying federally required overtime?

On-premises food service?

Will you offer on-premises food service that will require a cook, server, and dishwasher? These positions should be in addition to the tasting room staff to avoid increased risk of a bad customer experience. Does your building have a potential kitchen space that will permit installation of a mandatory exhaust hood and fan that vent to the outside? Do you want to be subject to regular health department inspections?

Production?

How much of the production will you be performing? Are you a brick-and-mortar winery, a virtual winery, or something in between? There is nothing wrong with any choice you make as long as you are honest about what can you do vs. what must be hired out.

What size of staff?

Do you have enough staff to manage your winery when someone quits or is dismissed? Do you have your own ready-to-go training program for new staff?

Wine club program?

To be successful, this program may require the full attention of an employee.

Conclusions

Look at my list of seven questions, some of which you'll need to substitute your product information for the words "wine" and "tasting room." Basically keep the balance between your job and your life: which is primary and which secondary. Do you work to support your lifestyle and is the price you pay reasonable, or do you need to adjust your lifestyle? Remember the concept of a lifestyle business; something we do because we want to and not because it necessarily maximizes our earnings potential. Remember to value the quality of life and to have a life after the inevitable end of your work day.

36. Interstate Shipping

General business points:
- **Legal limits**
- **Common carriers**
- **Licenses/fees**

In the fall of 2005, the U.S. Supreme Court case of Granholm v. Heald modified interstate shipping laws concerning the sale of wine. The Court's decision upheld the right of individual states to regulate the sale of beverage alcohol, but those regulations must be consistent with the Commerce Clause in the Ninth Amendment to the United States Constitution. States were instructed to refrain from creating any regulations that treated in-state wineries differently from out-of-state wineries in regards to the shipping of wine across state lines.

The Supreme Court's decision sounded like a victory for small wineries, and it probably would have been, except for the fact that many states are forever at odds with the specter of federal law. Remember, we are the country that fought a civil war in large part over the issue of state's rights.

After the decision, the federal government began telling all 50 states in what manner they could conduct a portion of their business. To almost no one's surprise, things did not turn out the way the small wineries hoped they would. The law did not specify exactly how individual states would create an environment of shipping equality. Some states such as Louisiana achieved compliance by disallowing ALL shipments of wine across their borders. According to the Supreme Court, these states were now treating all wineries the same.

Another unintended consequence of Granholm v. Heald involved reciprocal shipping states. Prior to the Court's decision, thirteen states allowed any licensed winery in one state to ship to customers in any of the other reciprocal states without acquiring additional state licenses. The reciprocal states now required all wineries to obtain a license to ship wine into their state. This system of licensing insured each state would receive the taxes they were due for wines sold to their citizens. The winery that was licensed to ship into a state would collect applicable state taxes from their customers and remit those taxes back to the customer's home state. The system worked reasonably well as taxes were collected with no loss of tax revenue due to out-of-state shipping. But small wineries suffered from a need to acquire licenses and fidelity bonds from each state where they shipped, including the old reciprocal states.

It's Not What You Make...

It's what you get to keep that counts.

This brings us to a third unintended consequence of Granholm v. Heald. After the Court's decision, states began using licensing fees as a means to block shipping by small, out-of-state wineries. How did this happen? License fees were often set at a point that made shipping to some states financially undesirable for small wineries. For example, in 2011 the license fee to ship into Connecticut is $1,000 per year. In Nebraska, it is $500 per year. That's a lot of money for a small winery. Other states, such as New York, created non-financial barriers by requiring that a winery's home state's licensing costs and rules match New York's state costs and rules exactly before an out-of-state winery could acquire a New York shipping license.

By 2011, either due to an outcry from their citizens or through some bit of rare wisdom by legislators, various states began attempts at standardizing license requirements and licensing language. The standardization of licenses is not yet complete, but when it is finalized, it should eliminate the disparity in interstate shipping.

Why was being licensed in individual states such a problem for me? After Granholm vs. Heald, I worked to acquire licensing in twenty-seven states. I passed on the more expensive states, such as Connecticut and Nebraska, but I applied for and received a license in all states with a fee equal to or less than $300 per year. Naturally, there were plenty of annoyances in acquiring and maintaining these licenses.

Out-of-State Taxes or Fees?

Before issuing a license, many states required the posting of a tax bond. Some of these states further required the bonding agent be located in state. Each state required me to file a written monthly accounting of all shipping to their state—even if there was no shipping in a given month. I had to pay individual state taxes every month and in some states I was required to break the tax payment down by the county in which customers resided. Some states, such as Montana and Ohio, required the resident who purchased my wines to also acquire a license in order to receive wine from an out-of-state winery. Pennsylvania allowed me to ship into their state, but I was only allowed to ship to state liquor stores where my customers would then pick up their purchases.

With so many regulations involved, I was forced to keep a folder with the rules for each and every state.

Despite these petty rules and requirements, I shipped my wines all over the country from 2005 until the end of 2007. At the end of 2007, I decided it was time to see if my shipping program and interstate wine club were making money.

On a state-by-state basis, I determined if my sales were profitable given the cost of the license bonding. As a way of measuring profit vs. cost, I analyzed my shipping totals using a minimum fifty percent profit figure on goods sold. For example, if I shipped less than $350 in sales to Arizona, according to the fifty percent profit figure I lost money on the annual state license fee of $175. In Texas, the figure for annual licensing and tax bonding was $250 per year, so $500 in annual sales was my break-even point. My analysis revealed that aside from four states—California, Idaho, Missouri, and Washington—I was losing money on out-of-state shipping.

When I began shipping across the country for my Wine of the Month Club, I wanted to serve as many states as possible. Knowing that my out-of-state accounts came with a built-in expense due to licensing fees and tax bonding, I implemented a series of cost-cutters to increase profitability. I created and maintained my own website and saved on shipping by sending out my wines on a quarterly instead of a monthly basis. As a customer incentive to increase purchases, I provided club members with recipe cards and, after their first year of club membership, included free wine accessories for my members.

And yet, despite all my frugality and membership incentives, the level of wine club business did not justify the license fees in most states. I determined that my Wine of the Month Club generated sales but not profits. My limited size made it difficult to profit when the aggregated costs of state licensing exceeded several thousand dollars per year. So in 2008, I cut my shipping to the non-profitable states and retained the four states where shipping was profitable.

I effectively closed my wine club to all but four states. Wine clubs are highly touted and very popular, but the facts are that for a small winery, operating a wine club that ships across a large number of states can be difficult.

Shipping with Common Carriers

To operate a wine club legally, you must be able to ship legally, which currently means getting licensed as a wine shipper by UPS, Federal Express, or DHL. In the future, the U.S. Post Office may also allow wine shipments, but for now you'll have to deal with the Big Three. To get licensed with these companies, you must be a shipping agent. This involves you paying a small monthly fee, or you can use a shipping agent on a fee-for-service basis. You must also buy and use approved shipping boxes.

There is the extra time and expense of having an employee individually check shipping costs for potential customers. Additionally, in my experience a wine club must present clear and simple costs for customer participation, which becomes difficult with different shipping rates to different states. Each of these issues is bothersome yet solvable, but you must always keep in mind the costs of packing, shipping, and record keeping for individual states.

Fulfillment Houses

In California, the wine industry can access businesses known as fulfillment houses. These are professional shipping and clearing houses that receive orders, package items, and ship parcels. A fulfillment house may ship flower bulbs, pots and pans, knives, books, or almost anything else you might buy online—and that includes wine. The fulfillment houses are fee-for-service operations that provide a good value if you operate your wine club in a major marketing area. California-based wine clubs can more easily and more profitably ship wines by using fulfillment houses, allowing them to generate profits in a larger number of states. As a result, California wine clubs are free to offer their customers a variety of wine brands instead of being tied to a single winery. The ability to offer a greater variety of brands solves a persistent wine club problem—small wineries often run through their available product line in a relatively short period of time, leaving customers with little incentive to continue their subscription.

In summary, despite my experiences, I believe wine clubs can be profitable. I feel the keys to success are having a large enough club membership to justify a dedicated staff member and multiple state license fees. Bigger is better, at least with wine club membership rolls.

A New, Better Approach to Wine Clubs

The best winery in our county has 3 wine club options. Their clubs provide discounts and other perks to club members but the member must pick up their required purchases from the winery. Brilliant! I hope they got the idea from the first printing of my book, but in any case their clubs are successful and don't involve interstate shipping.

Getting Discovered by out-of-State Customers

My wine club experience wasn't all bad. In time, I received an email pitch from a Windsor, California distributorship that I'll call a hybrid distributorship/fulfillment house—in other words, a direct marketing service. Zero Link Markets, Inc. and I enjoyed a long and profitable relationship. Basically, ZLM created VinoShipper.com, which in 2011 was licensed to ship to about twenty-five states. They advertise online as the representative of wineries throughout the country. Visitors to their website could search by winery name, state, or grape variety. Each winery that VinoShipper represents sets its own retail prices, case discounts, and shipper costs, which in turn are displayed on the VinoShipper site. VinoShipper makes an online sale to a customer, then emails the winery a copy of the order, packing list, and UPS shipping label.

My relationship with VinoShipper consisted of drop-shipping products to customers on VinoShipper's behalf while making a legal sale to ZLM, a California distributorship. The cost to me was twelve percent on the goods sold. VinoShipper did all the advertising, collected from the customer, and sent my payment—minus commission—via direct deposit each month. To take advantage of their service, I only needed a license to sell to my distributor—ZLM—in California. Eventually, VinoShipper also acquired a license to serve as my distributor to trade accounts in California.

These remarks about VinoShipper are not intended as an advertisement for one particular service provider. I just use them as an example to remind you to review your options for shipping and marketing help. Remember to weigh the options and seek the best balance between "price worthy" and "hassle free" for your particular set of circumstances.

Conclusions

Whatever you ship may be subject to particular rules. Hazardous material, explosives, biomedical and radioactive goods would be broad categories with specific federal and state rules. Similarly, does your product require paying state taxes or needing state bonding at the destination? Do your finished goods or raw materials need to be shipped refrigerated or are the goods unstackable, because they will crush, so they will take up more floor space in a trailer than stackable goods?

Think about delivery expenses as a factor in the total price paid by your customer. Do the shipping expenses make the product non-competitive in the customer's market? If so, then your choices are to look for cheaper alternate shipping methods, such as rail or trucks that are dead-heading back empty. Remember it's the delivered cost of the goods that matters to the customer.

Can you use a fulfillment-house-type operation or regional warehouses to lessen shipping costs?

37. Tasting Charges, Corkage, By-The-Glass Pricing

General business points:
- **Sampling**
- **Portion size**
- **Corkage**

When I opened my tasting room, I allowed anyone to taste anything they wanted for free. This turned out to be a mistake. Since I made more than twenty styles of wine, the unrestricted tasting was expensive and time-consuming. Worst of all, my generosity did not generate increased sales. When I inevitably started designing a new and improved tasting system, I first considered having specific wines available to taste on a particular day. I dismissed this idea since my selection was large and the preferences of my customers tended to vary. I decided to give one taste for free and then charge a small fee to taste four more wines. In effect, a visitor could taste five wines for $1. If they wanted to try more than five wines, I added an extra charge of $1 per taste.

This new system was very successful for one simple reason: If a customer knows he has a limited number of choices, he will review his options more carefully and only try those wines that are genuinely of interest to him, thereby eliminating the frivolous tasting that ate into my profits. The extra tasting charge, which I could—and often would—waive as a "feel good" for customers, kept the number of free tastings at an acceptable level. The limit of five wines per customer also significantly shortened the time required to conduct the average tasting.

To further assist the customer and the employees, we provided printed price lists and pencils for the customers to use in selecting which wines they wanted to taste. It was an advantage for staff to be handed a printed list that was annotated with the selected wines. Staff could pull from the cooler and put in the correct order the wines that any one taster or one group desired.

Researching Where to Set My By-the-Glass Prices

I set the by-the-glass prices for my wines after doing two bits of research. First, I surveyed the market at local restaurants for their by-the-glass prices on key varieties. The second bit of research involved pour sizes. The size of my pours turned out to be a somewhat difficult decision. If the price of a glass of Merlot was $6, was that for a five, six or eight ounce pour? A 750 ml bottle equals 25.4 ounces, so those servings are good pour size choices, equating to five, four or three servings per bottle, respectively. Eventually I settled on a pour size of six ounces.

Pour Size is Portion Control

In determining my pour size, I needed to find some way for my staff to easily and accurately hit the target pour size at every serving. Fortunately for me I had previously decided to use a tasting room glass with our winery name lithographed in a horizontal band around the center of the glass. This logo gave my staff a visible pour mark to use. Filling the glass to the bottom of the logo measured exactly six ounces. I therefore based my by-the-glass prices on what comparable wines at comparable pour sizes were selling for.

Because I served a larger variety of wines than was customary on restaurant by-the-glass menus, sometimes I needed to adjust my strategy of surveying local restaurant prices for use in determining my prices. On wines with no readily available price comparison, I set my price by using similarly priced restaurant bottles of different varieties. Since I sold the only Lemberger by-the-glass wine in my area, I used my bottle price of $15 to find a comparably priced wine on a restaurant wine list, and then used that comparable wine to fix my by-the-glass price at $6. This system gave some internal consistency within my price lists for bottles or glasses. I also used this strategy for corkage charges.

Corkage Fees

Corkage is the fee charged for the privilege of opening a bottle of wine that you bring into a restaurant. In our tasting room, I charged corkage on bottles that customers purchased in the tasting room and then took into the wine bar to drink. Tasting room retail prices were set to be competitive with retail store prices as opposed to retail restaurant prices. Store prices generally are based on a thirty percent mark-up while restaurant prices are based on a minimum of 100% mark-up. Having a wine bar in my tasting room meant that I had to deal with two very common, but very different, profit margins.

You might wonder why I didn't just forego corkage on my own bottles. The reason is the significantly larger overhead involved when you have on-premises consumption: extra licensing, increased liability insurance, more glassware, and cleanup of tables and floors. In general, the price for a bottle of wine is much lower than the equivalent cost of purchasing the same amount of wine by the glass. If I didn't have a small corkage charge, I would be undercutting my own by-the-glass program once customers realized they could purchase a bottle of wine from my retail space and then drink it in my wine bar at a lower cost than by-the-glass purchases. I charged $5 per bottle corkage, which created a more acceptable ratio between the by-the-glass and by-the-bottle price without meeting any customer resistance.

Let's look at an example. A $16 bottle of Merlot equals a bit more than four glasses of six-ounce pours. The cost of four glasses is $24. If I sell bottle quantities in my by-the-glass wine bar at the by-the-bottle tasting room price, four glasses equals $4 per glass, I have the added expenses of running a wine bar with none of the added profits. The corkage charge shrinks the gap between the glass and bottle prices.

Conclusions

Product sampling is never free, so develop policies and controls to guide how it's done. For example, when I sampled a wholesale customer, I didn't leave a sample bottle. It might be given away instead of being tasted. I tasted with the customer and answered questions then took the remainder of the bottle with me.

Sampling at my tasting room, or in the sales office, for retail customers is an industry practice. Accept the expense and include it in your overhead. I limited my tasting costs by imposing a minimal charge. I also established a hybrid sample program called wine flights. These are pours larger than free sample but smaller than glass servings. The customer chose between groups of wines presented in different flight options. Look to create your own options that both promote tasting but minimize your costs. In both the above circumstances, portion control on the pour size was central. You need to know how much you are giving away, as an advertising expense, to capture the sampling costs in your overhead.

Corkage is perhaps unique to on-sale beer and wine businesses. Corkage prevents someone running the numbers in their head and then figuring a work-around to drink more cheaply on your premises. Without a corkage charge I believe a wine-by-the-glass program would quickly die.

38.   Selling Beer in the Wine Bar

General business points:
- **Expanding on-premises options**
- **Listening to the market place**
- **Updating training**

When my wine bar opened, I quickly discovered a need to jump into the beer business. Why? What I had not anticipated was groups of customers who came into the wine bar with at least one member of the group being a beer drinker. The group dynamic intended that each member of the group receive their favorite type of beverage. If I had no beer to offer the beer drinker, the entire group would leave for the neighboring pool parlor where everybody could drink their favorite beverage. The pool parlor offered mass-produced American beers and lower-tier wines, but that was enough to satisfy each and every group member. If I wanted to keep these groups as repeat customers instead of watching them traipse off to the pool parlor, I had to offer a selection of beers.

Are You Selling a Perishable Product?

My first beer offering consisted of a mix of microbrews and popular imports such as Pacifico and Guinness. I soon realized, through painful experience, that microbrews are rarely pasteurized, which gives them a shelf life of about four months. I threw out lots of skunky, micro-brewed beers. The skunky quality that develops is caused by methyl-anthranilate, which some beer drinkers find unique and desirable. Most beer drinkers find it undesirable.

Imported beers are all pasteurized and have a shelf life starting at twelve months and increasing as the alcohol content increases. While microbrews are always sold in twenty-four-bottle cases, imports are often sold in smaller case packs starting as low as eight bottles per pack. The longer shelf life and smaller case units make it possible to offer a greater selection of beers with fewer spoilage issues. I found that by staying with imported beers that were not common to grocery store shelves, there was also less price resistance from customers. At the time I retired, I had ninety-three varieties of imported beer available. Beer sales accounted for nineteen percent of my cash flow. My profit margin on beers started at 100% markup. Having beers available also significantly enhanced my catering service options.

When choosing your beer options, remember that beer is sensitive to ultra-violate light. Clear glass bottles and green glass bottles are inferior to brown glass bottles when it comes to keeping beer fresh. Even aluminum cans are superior to clear or green bottles. For your purposes, it may be wise to stock beers in either brown glass or aluminum cans.

Best Selection in Idaho!

A new marketing option created.

My menu grew until I could advertise having the largest selection of imported beers in northern Idaho. But now I faced the problem of a daunting selection for the average beer consumer. In answer to this problem, I tried arranging beers by country of origin, then by style—lagers with lagers and stouts with stouts—until I finally discovered that the best method for my customers was to arrange the beers by color. Sorting by color also dodged the problem of beers vs. ales, a "distinction without a difference" based on the brewer's choice of top or bottom fermenting yeasts.

This method of sorting by color also avoided the problem of having black lagers mixed in with American lagers that look like a glass of Coors. Later, I amplified the information for the customer by adding a shelf description for each and every beer. These brief descriptions allowed the customer to distinguish between the styles that sat side-by-side in color groups. The descriptions were maintained on a spreadsheet. As beers were shifted to other spots, items dropped, or new beers were added, we could easily update the description sheets.

Keeping Staff Current on New Products

Writing the beer descriptions became a training opportunity as my staff and I sampled new beers as a team and created the descriptions. As I introduced my staff to a new beer, I also informed them about other beers that were similar in taste or style. A single, shared beer geometrically increased their product knowledge. It taught them which beers and ales had a similar taste or style without the added expense of allowing each staff member to sample each and every beer. The empty bottle from the shared beer then went into our window display as a draw to passers-by.

As a further benefit to my beer-drinking customers, I offered beer discounts that matched the discounts given on wine. I also started a beer 'preferred customer card program.'

Conclusions

One operational change may suggest other changes that you have not considered. Keep in mind the duality of product and service. Have what the customers want, as far as is possible. Group behavior becomes a factor if you can't meet the needs/desires of the entire group. As changes take place we must update our training to keep staff current on product information and procedures. This is also a wonderful time to include staff input on your decision-making process. Every entrepreneur I have ever met is a 'Type A' personality. A 'Type A' is smart, driven, confident and able to make decisions. Don't let your self-confidence close you off to other people's ideas, suggestions or input. Even a 'Type A' needs to listen more and talk less.

39. Offering Sparkling Wine

General business points:
- **Expanding the product line**
- **Equipment issues**

There may come a time, as the owner of a small winery, where you begin to see a need to offer your own brand of sparkling wines. With a winery operating in a town that contained a major university and with another major university only eight miles away, it soon became evident that I would need to offer sparkling wine. The endless parade of mothers and fathers arriving for graduations and weddings meant I needed a steady supply of sparklers.

Previously I mentioned that a salesperson can sometimes get customers to change from one variety of red wine to another. However, you can't get someone who wants sparkling wine to consider a still wine as an acceptable substitute for a wedding toast!

Once I decided to offer sparkling wine, I approached my mentor, who generously shared his formula for re-fermenting a base wine (cuvée) into a sparkler. Adding to the knowledge of sparklers I'd already acquired from my previous time working with Mr. Kruse, I now learned the process of disgorging. This tricky process involves the removing of sediments from a bottle of sparkling wine after re-fermentation. I also learned about dosage (finishing the disgorged wine with sugar and alcohol) and the corking of sparkling wines.

Developing New Products

A new learning curve.

Now it was time to create my own sparklers. To create these wines, I would need a bottleneck chiller, a larger pre-chiller unit, a cuvée blending tank, a tank mixer, and a set of riddling racks.

As I've described before, many non-specialty winemaking items are entirely serviceable for a winery's equipment needs.

Meeting New Equipment Needs by Adapting

A steam kettle placed on a stand became a cuvée tank with gravity flow to a bottling machine. Even tank mixers can be replaced by a simple canoe paddle. Before I could afford an electric tank mixer, my young son stood on a ladder and continually stirred the cuvée wine, sugar, nutrients, and adjuvant blend with a canoe paddle while I bottled the cuvée.

I also needed a beer-capping machine, since sparkling wine is first capped while it re-ferments and is not corked until later. When champagne production had grown sufficiently, my hobby-sized hand capper was replaced with a semi-automatic capping machine.

Once the cuvée is rebottled, it is allowed to re-ferment for several months. After it has re-fermented, the sediments inside the bottles are compacted prior to removal. The compaction process, called riddling, is essentially a way to settle the sediments into the neck of the bottle where they form a single plug. For my riddling process, I had a series of riddling racks built out of plywood and installed along the walls of a storage room. This racking system allowed me to riddle twenty cases of wine at one time.

Riddling can be performed in large, expensive machines called gyro-pallets or by hand in riddling racks. When sales justified the expense, I upgraded my riddling capacity, also lessening the physical strain on me, by having a non-automated riddling machine constructed. The machine looked much like a children's playground merry-go-round. This allowed me to riddle more bottles by rotating the machine twice a day for 2 weeks.

Once the sediment inside the bottle is compacted into the neck, it is removed in a process called disgorging. Chilling reduces the internal pressure in the bottles, allowing the champagne master to remove the sediment without losing the sparkle.

For my winery, a large chest freezer with an added thermostat served as a pre-chiller. Initially I finished the disgorging process in a small stainless steel vessel partially filled with acetone that I chilled by adding dry ice. It was slow, but cheap and effective. When product justified the expense, I went to a small chest freezer fitted with a locally made galvanized pan as my bottle chiller.

Then I finished the bottle to the desired sweetness through the dosage processes. Dosage is the process of topping the disgorged bottle to the proper fill level by adding a small amount of sugar syrup. The volume and sweetness of the syrup is changed to produce finished sparkling wines of different dryness.

After disgorging and dosage, the final processes of corking and caging are accomplished. You can choose to use a special corking machine (current cost of $6,000) and sparkling wine corks (current cost of $0.50 apiece), or you can go the cheaper and more profitable route. For my sparkling wines, I sealed my finished bottles with a plastic stopper (current cost of $0.05 apiece) that I pounded into the bottle with a rubber mallet. While not as classy as a cork, bottles finished with manual corking and plastic stoppers illustrate the choices that can make a business more profitable.

Another Route into the Champagne Business

If, after reading about my efforts to create sparkling wine, you want no part of it, fear not! Just as you can buy bulk wine or even unlabeled, already-bottled wines called shiners, so too can you find unlabeled sparklers. If you buy from another producer before the product is disgorged, you can label the sparkler as produced and bottled by YOU! This is a nice way to maximize your cache of sparklers. Remember that by buying someone else's work you are choosing to forego the valued added portion of potential profit. Instead of producing your sparklers at the lower cost of just purchasing, crushing, and fermenting grapes yourself, you are now paying someone else to provide you with an almost-finished sparkling wine. Additionally, make sure that the TTB rules about who is listed as the producer have not changed since this writing.

Adding a Flourish as a Marketing Tool

My final, crowning touch to becoming the only producer of hand-made sparkling wine in Idaho was learning to sabrage bottles. Sabrage is the technique of opening sparkling wine bottles with a sword strike that cleanly removes the cork and bottle neck. My sabrage was an act of pure theater that I could perform at caterings. Done properly and safely it is way cool! Learn, practice, and be careful as you are dealing with a sword and a razor-sharp bottle neck.

I have one last note about sparklers. Contrary to legend, Dom Pierre Perignon, the Dominican cellar master, did not perfect or invent the making of sparkling wines. Quite the contrary; the story is largely a marketing myth created by the Moet Champagne House. Dom Perignon actually spent his days in the cold cellars at Hautvillers trying to prevent his quality table wine from re-fermenting. Sparkling wine was considered to be "The Devil's Wine" by Dom Perignon.

Conclusions

As new product lines are added, new equipment needs arise. Adapt, borrow, rent, if you can. Remember, it is the use of specialized equipment that is needed, not the ownership. Ownership engenders cost, storage space and maintenance; avoid them if you can.

Especially consider product changes that open added marketing opportunities. By adding sparkling wines, I enhanced my chances of selling to wedding parties and other celebrations. I added marketing touches such as sabrage to enhance the appeal of both my product and service.

Small changes/additions/course corrections are preferable to big changes in your operation. When the opportunity for cost effective change presents itself, review your training and sales practices. Remember, whatever we make must be sold.

40. Wine: Easy to Make, Hard to Sell

General business points:

- **Enhance profits and lower price by minimizing packaging costs**

As previously discussed, there are several business models for wineries: the brick-and-mortar winery and the various hybrid options that are all or in-part virtual wineries. The hybrid and virtual wineries exchange value-added profits for simplicity of operation, but they do not necessarily increase sales or profitability.

One of my favorite movies is 'Space Balls', a Star Wars satire. The Lone Star, a takeoff on Luke Skywalker, encounters the film's version of the Yoda character—called Yogurt and played by Mel Brooks—and learns about The Force (called The Schwartz in Space Balls). Yogurt takes Lone Star to a closet to show him The Schwartz. When opened, the closet is full of 'Space Balls' movie merchandise—backpacks, binders, lunch boxes, etc. Yogurt then tells Lone Star about The Schwartz "...everything is merchandising." These words are true even in the wine business.

As you know by now, my winery was a value-added winery. It made money by taking raw materials and turning them into finished products. This is a prime example of value added, but value added is not the only way to make money.

Refillable Bottles

One of the more ingenious selling devices I have seen is used by a hybrid winery and a bricks-and-mortar winery, both in northern Idaho. Packaging—bottle, cork, label, neck foil— typically represent about 40% of the cost in a typical 750 ml bottle of premium wine. Having a reusable bottle program allows the 40% savings to be split between the producer and retail customer.

The hybrid winery makes most of its own wine but also acquires, bottles, and sells two purchased wines—one red and one white—under its own label. The purchased wines represent the low end of their product line, but these two wines are good values. Both wines were profitable additions to the winery's portfolio. The bricks-and mortar winery makes all the wine they sell. They offer a changing variety of red or white wines in their own refillable bottles.

I'll call these reusable bottle programs "Bring Your Own Bottle" The BYOB concept involves selling wine at the tasting room in bottles that have a permanent lithographed label for the two wines that are the BYOB choices. The lithographed permanent labels satisfy the TTB rule, which requires that wine sold to retail customers be in a labeled bottle. The first time a customer purchases a BYOB wine, they're actually buying both the wine and the BYOB bottle. Going forward, the customer needs only return the BYOB bottle and have it refilled. The refilling of these returned bottles puts the responsibility for cleaning the bottle on the customer. The refilled bottle is recorked. Refilling can be done while the customer waits because the BYOB wines are available on tap.

Conclusions

Packaging and shipping are significant contributors to product cost. Seek means to lower your costs without sacrificing quality or profits. Growlers in beer and reusable bottles for wine are two such examples. You lower your cost and split the savings with the customer so everybody wins!

As mentioned before, everything we make must be sold. Always look for options that advance you and enhance the ultimate salability of your product.

41. Wine Competitions, Awards and Medals

General business points:
- **Cost to benefits of awards**
- **National vs. local**

I entered my wines in a large number of wine competitions. I believed critics and peers could validate my credibility as a winemaker. For pure marketing purposes, this was a decent tactic. But as the years wore on and I learned more about the true working of various wine festivals, I began to modify my approach. My biggest modifications were spurred by two subtle lessons I learned about wine competitions—cost-to-benefit and national vs. local.

I learned the cost-to-benefit lesson when I discovered that some wine festivals have a lower level of credibility in the eyes of the industry. While victories in these competitions may gain you a valuable, but temporary, marketing tool, it's important to identify these festivals and avoid them. It's kind of like the old joke about peeing in your pants in a dark suit—it gives you a nice warm feeling but nobody notices. If you enter and attend these festivals, you will spend a significant sum of money to get a disproportionately small amount of recognition.

How Much Fame Can You Afford?

Some festivals are designed with categories that are probably not a good fit for your product line. You should pass on these. There are competitions that require your wines to be available for sale in the festival's geographic area. If you don't have a license in that area, you can't enter your wines in the competition.

Nearly all competitions, especially the major festivals, are fundraising events for a fair or service organization. Consequently, they are NOT free. Bottom line: only enter competitions that suit your product line and where the potential for valuable marketing recognition exceeds the cost of entry and attendance.

Being Judged Is *Not* Free

Festivals and competitions are an advertising expense. Having a medal from a prestigious event allows you to advertise the award and/or affix an award sticker on your bottles. That said, the question now becomes, "How much fame can you afford?"

For example, the most price-worthy of the four major competitions is the Los Angeles County Fair. Cost, in 2011, was $75 per entry. The deadline for submitting wines is May, with the judging staged in June. At your own expense, you ship six bottles of each entry to the competition headquarters. Then, if you win a gold medal, you are obligated to sell up to twenty-four bottles of the award-winning wine, at your wholesale price, to the competition hosts. If you choose to enter more wines, you have to pay more entry fees. Multiply the entry fee and cost of shipping by four, six, eight, or ten entries and you can see the enormous annual expense associated with just one competition. And the L.A. competition is the least costly of the four major events I mentioned! So as you see, a wine judging at a venue that matters is not cheap. Keep in mind the cost-to-benefit ratio of trying to win medals.

Here's a final analogy. Wine competitions—whether national or regional—can be likened to a fishing license. You get a chance to try your luck with no guarantee of success. If only I could buy a catching license rather than a fishing license!

National Vs. Local

Experience taught me that small, regional wineries are equally benefited by the most credible regional competitions. Your local marketing efforts will be enhanced from these regional competitions as well as from skipping some of the national competitions. What you lose in "fame" from skipping the national judgings will be more than made up for by the impact to your sales from credible, regional competitions.

Having national medals to display in my tasting room assisted with on-premises sales. Awards and recognition from regional events boosted restaurant and store sales because festival attendees were introduced to wines that they could then find in their local market.

My strategy, developed over years, was to choose two national competitions and some local events to get the best mix of tangible benefits. For recognition purposes, I narrowed my list of judgings to the events held annually in Dallas and Los Angeles. For local marketing purposes, I participated in two regional events—one in Boise, Idaho, and the other in Tri-Cities, Washington. If I had to pay a fee for a chance to receive recognition or increased sales, I wanted the biggest bang for my buck—and you should, too!

Conclusions

Advertising comes in many different forms, commercial judging being one. Evaluate the options in your business arena with an eye toward the cost-to-benefit ratio of entering. Commercial awards serve to introduce you to an industry and give a new business credibility, but not on an ever-increasing basis, in my opinion. Pick your competitions for the prestige of a potential win. Some contest wins provide national recognition while others only have local value.

42.   Where to Advertise

General business points:
- **Market analysis**
- **Advertising strategies**

My favorite quote about advertising comes from the founder of the Philadelphia-based Wanamaker's Department Store chain who said, "I believe I'm wasting half of my advertising budget. I just don't know which half." While it's couched in a joke, this statement is actually good advice. A small business owner must remain logical and vigilant where advertising is concerned.

Advertising for a small winery is seldom, if ever, a call to action for the consumer. It's a rare person who will read a wine ad, watch a wine commercial, or see a wine billboard and then run to their local tasting room to purchase a bottle.

In my experience, the advertising medium that works best for a small winery is the one that's the best fit for consumers who are already wine customers. The relative price-worthiness of the various advertising options must be considered before expending any funds. Advertising is necessary for any business, but the amount of funds you allocate to your ad budget is just as important as where you choose to spend those funds.

Discovering Who Your Real Customers Are

Directing your advertising.

Over time I discovered that my tasting room customers were tourists, visitors to town, or local folks bringing in their out-of-town guests. The local populace, on the other hand, was more likely to purchase individual bottles of my wine from local stores.

Once I was armed with this understanding of who actually made up my customer base, an advertising plan emerged. I had my best luck attracting tourists by advertising with in-room motel directories, Chamber of Commerce visitor's guides, and regional visitor's guides. I want to place a special emphasis on the regional visitor's guides as a means to reach out-of-towners. In Idaho, and perhaps your state, tax money from the Department of Commerce is disbursed to regional tourism councils who in turn publish and distribute tourism directories for their parts of the state. These directories are a commonly read item among tourists, which makes them an ideal place to advertise for out-of-town customers.

Understanding that a lot of my customers were wine tourists also led me to use the regional wine consumers publication as an advertising vehicle. I did this by regularly submitting wine samples for the magazine's review. As you read in the very beginning of this book, I "routinely received praise from Wine Press Northwest magazine—typically in their 'Best Buy' section." The Northwest Wine Press readership consisted of wine lovers who valued the magazine's recommendations. Their validation of my wine as price worthy made the cost of samples and postage money well spent.

Of course, not all tourists are visiting from hundreds of miles away and reading through regional directories. I did a regular and significant amount of business with people who lived within my geographical region and were simply on an outing with their spouse or friends. These folks might be out for a day's drive or an overnight getaway, making my winery a tourist destination for them. This group of customers was better reached by local TV advertising. The TV advertising budget worked best by spending money on selective sponsorship of shows such as "Exploring the Northwest," a regional travel program.

I also came to realize sales to distributors are a form of advertising. Sales to distributors, while less profitable per unit than selling directly to retailers or customers in a tasting room, generate a larger number of overall sales. Through these distributors, customers saw my products on store shelves. This lent an air of credibility to my wines that I might otherwise have lacked if I sold only through my tasting room.

Radio Advertising Strategy

On occasion, I purchased radio advertising in my local community. Toward the end of the calendar year, a two-month advertising blitz on local radio promoted a winter specialty wine. This radio advertising featured thirty-second spots that I wrote and recorded. Following the advice of an advertising executive, my ads were broadcast in a road-block format. Road-block advertising means that instead of having the same number of ads every day, your spots are grouped with multiple ads on some days and no ads running on other days. The thinking here is that you can increase the likelihood that any individual listener will hear your advertisement by increasing the number of chances he or she has to hear your ad on a single day. Remember, the generally agreed upon key to successful radio or TV advertising is repetition, repetition, and repetition.

On-Premises Advertising

The final type of advertising to consider is on-premises advertising, such as signage. Signs are a one-time advertising expense that can pay great dividends. If you are spending money on other forms of advertising to get people into your winery, shouldn't they be able to find you? Clear signage at eye level is the key. Signs that are above eye level are often overlooked, especially if there are trees in front of the building.

A good way to overcome the limits of overhead signage is with decals on the outside of your street-level windows. For my winery, I used gold leaf decals that horizontally displayed "Camas Prairie Winery" across every window. I also had the winery name in twenty-four-inch-tall raised plastic letters placed higher up on the front of the building. Unfortunately, I learned the hard way about signage above eye level being generally overlooked. A final note about signage: remember to check with your town about sign ordinances that limit the total amount of visible signage.

Don't ignore your window space as a form of advertisement! Storefronts are designed to allow for displays that give passers-by a quick visual exhibit about your products. In my windows, I had a large display of imported beers. We used empty beer bottles for the window display, so there was no cost involved beyond the display rack. I also kept the windows uncluttered so people passing by could see we had tables for wine and beer by the glass. I limited the number of posters and flyers that I put on the doors and windows. I had clearly posted days and hours of operation, along with an emergency contact number on the same sign.

Finally, and perhaps most importantly, I NEVER displayed signs for political candidates or for social issues. Posters and flyers were not allowed on the doors and windows. No matter on which side of the political spectrum you fall, roughly half of your potential customers are on the other side. It just makes sense to avoid signs that might actually turn some people away.

Website

As the population gets younger and more tech-savvy, the importance of a good Internet site increases. Most towns have local website designers who can set up your site with all the usual elements: home page, hours of operation, promotional pictures, and product lists.

For my site, I added pull-down connections for information on our Wine 101 class, catering services, custom labeling options (including sample label pictures), and pricing details. Our Wine-of-the-Month Club was accessible, too, with separate pages on customer options, an index of shipping costs for all 27 states to which I was licensed to ship, and a printable enrollment form. There was a pull-down that also showed and explained our environmental efforts, such as solar power and my exclusive use of lightweight wine bottles. My successor, being more internet-savvy and more energetic, has updated the winery website with information on in-house live music events and new product releases.

Conclusions

Hopefully your product is so good that you'll need an unlisted phone number and address to manage the hoards of eager buyers. If not, then advertising is a necessary investment, but one with no bottom to the amount of money you can pour in. Find out who is actually your target market and tailor your advertising to them in terms of selecting where and how to spend your money. Whether it's through trade journals, chambers of commerce, tourist bureaus, media, or on-premises signage, track the return on your dollars and adjust future spending accordingly.

43.   Green Marketing

General business points:
- **Marketing strategy**

Over the years, I learned that stealing good ideas was easier than thinking of the ideas myself. Feel free to steal ideas from this book! In the case of green marketing, I built upon some common sense business practices with cost-saving and environmentally conscious concepts. I began using lightweight glass bottles because they were cheaper to buy and ship than heavier bottles. A lightweight bottle weighs about eight ounces. A heavyweight bottle can weigh twenty ounces. It takes energy to melt glass and energy to move glass from factory, to distributor, to winery, and to customer. More weight translates to more energy, which means more costs for natural gas for glass ovens and diesel fuel for shipping. Notwithstanding my own genuine environmental concerns, I first saw the lighter bottles as a cost-saver. Similarly, I used hot steam for winery sanitation because it was clean, produced on-contact sterilization of equipment, and left no chemical footprint.

Going further, we insulated every pipe in the winery, used only double-glazed glass in my remodeling efforts, updated furnaces and air conditioning with high efficiency products, and put timers on area lights and signage.

I researched solar power, learned my actual energy use rates from our public utility, and found a reputable vendor with good product knowledge. We then applied for and received a federal Renewable Energy Grant and installed a 5-kilowatt system for the winery in order to cut my huge energy bill. In 2008 the first of two solar arrays was installed.

We replaced our industrial-sized water heater with an on-demand water heater. For even more energy efficiency the hot water system used a circulating pump on a timer that turned off between midnight and 5 A.M. We got almost instant-on hot water without the waste of several gallons every time we turned on the hot water tap.

Finally, I took all the good, environmentally-friendly changes I had made and put them together as an advertising vehicle to position myself as Idaho's "green winery." These advertising rewards included multiple television appearances for my projects because Idaho's senior U.S. Senator toured my winery to see the results. I applied for and received an award as one of Idaho's Pollution Prevention Champions. I created a PowerPoint presentation that was uploaded to my website, detailing our actions and describing the subsequent environmental and financial benefits.

As you can see, being environmentally conscious can actually save you money, and it also makes a great angle for advertising your business. In this way, everybody wins!

Conclusions

Notwithstanding climate change deniers, green marketing worked for me. Green marketing can give you actual cost benefits and set you apart from your competition. Being business friendly and environmentally friendly are not mutually exclusive. Try to do both things for the good of your bottom line and future generations.

44.   Marketing Groups and Co-Promotion

General business points:
- **Marketing groups**
- **Paid marketing staff**

There are many regional wine associations that promote themselves as tourist destinations. Very smart! During the first twenty years of my winery's existence, I was the only winery within a 90-mile radius. Folks passing through town, people visiting family members in town, and students at one of three nearby colleges were pleasantly surprised to discover a good winery in such an unexpected place. But while I had no competition, I also had no power to draw a wine lover into my area—90 miles is just too far to travel to visit a single winery.

Marketing Groups

By 2005, there were four new wineries in the Palouse and Clearwater River Valley area. I approached these wineries and about seven grape growers with the idea of starting a regional marketing association. I approached the local growers because while they do not represent the public face of the wine business, they are the inseparable siblings of wineries. Growers must have a reliable market for their fruit, and wineries must have a reliable source of good grapes to make our good wines. The wineries, along with six of the seven growers, helped launch the new marketing association.

As a selling point, our marketing association noted that five wineries within a thirty-mile radius gave wine lovers a viable reason to make the drive to our area. We developed, printed, and distributed a two-sided rack card that displayed an area map on one side (with expanded views of each business location) and the name, address, phone number, and hours of operation for each member winery on the other side. This was simple, cheap, and effective advertising for everyone.

Within the first eighteen months, our association used up all of our rack cards and needed to print more! By this time, another winery had opened in the area. The new winery joined our association, as did the other local grower who had not previously joined. We now had six wineries and seven growers. We were on our way!

At this point, we'd reached a critical stage in the development of our marketing group. The rack cards had been a success and new members had joined. I also suggested we consider asking three local microbreweries if they would like to join our group.

We also had three new marketing ideas presented to the group: a wine glass passport program, a winery/brewery tour via bus or limo for local hotel or convention visitors, and a members-only website for buying, selling, and trading of equipment or components. Our group's incorporation was then in progress as was our IRS filings to obtain 501 (c) (6) status as a business league, which is what designates you as a tax-exempt promotional organization and allows you to do certain activities for the group. Clearly, our little marketing group was on the verge of becoming a huge success.

The Need for a Paid Staff

In the first meeting with our expanded group of six wineries, we established a marketing committee of two wineries and one grape grower. Alas, this is where the good news ends. Two members of the marketing committee were too busy to act on new ideas. The next meeting of our group failed to get scheduled, and two microbreweries were never asked to join our group. As a result, four member wineries eventually produced their own individual rack cards and the marketing group passed out of active existence.

So how did things go so wrong? In a word: TIME. Most of the wineries were part-time producers. The combined demands of their regular jobs in conjunction with the making of wine, operating a tasting room, and the selling of wine were too much. For these part-timers, it was sometimes easier to throw money at advertising or promotional issues than it was to spend the more precious currency of time.

Prior to our wine marketing association, I had also been involved with several volunteer marketing associations of downtown merchants. These groups—noble in purpose and price-worthy in membership costs—only went so far in their promotional efforts because operators of small businesses often lacked the time to grow the effort. This is why a paid Chamber of Commerce staff is vital to a business community. I am now convinced that a small regional winery, grower, and brewery marketing association must have dues-paying members and one or more paid staff.

As of the spring of 2019, a new revitalized trade group has formed, grown, and shown its worth over the past three years. What made this group successful, unlike its predecessor? The group wisely partnered with local Chambers of Commerce and the State Tourism Bureau, and used Community Economic Development Association (CEDA) grants. The marketing group hired a paid director and applied for every possible grant. It worked! The trade group co-promotes Idaho tourism and local community events and stages its own events.

Conclusions

In your particular field, try to recognize common interests with other producers. It might be marketing your location as a destination, so partner with the local Chamber(s) of Commerce. You might have access to a regional or national trade group that promotes your products. The U.S. government also promotes U.S. product abroad. Try to find co-promotion opportunities.

45.   Grapes

General business points:
- **Getting the best raw materials**
- **Cost-benefit ratios for labor**

Much of what I've presented in this book concerns ways to save money when operating a small winery. You can adapt equipment, you can use oak alternatives instead of purchasing barrels, and you can rent occasionally used equipment rather than buying it. But never, ever attempt to save money on grapes! The quality of your product will never surpass the quality of your raw materials. You can make bad wine out of good grapes, but you can't make good wine out of bad grapes!

Depending on where you are in your winemaking career—still planning or actually doing—you will likely find the cost of the wine in the bottle is about half of the packaging costs and assignable overhead on that same bottle. Buy good grapes!

I was lucky enough to source my grapes from the premier growers in Washington State. I got most of my grapes from Paul Champoux in the Horse Heaven Hills American Viticultural Area (AVA). What grape varieties Paul didn't grow, I sourced from two respected winery/growers that were producing Estate Grown (grown and produced by the same entity) wines from their own fruit.

Be a Good Customer

As a small fry among the client lists of these respected growers, I had to present myself as a desirable customer. Understand that it is easier for a grower to deal with one customer who buys fifty tons of grapes than to deal with five customers who purchase ten tons each. I made myself desirable as a customer by being easy to deal with and reliable. I ordered my grapes well in advance, usually in January. I never cancelled a grape order, leaving a grower holding the proverbial bag. I always showed up on time and with all my equipment ready to go. Because I needed to field crush, I cleaned up after myself. I never bounced a check. I never haggled about a price. I did everything to build long-term relationships with growers and did nothing that made me seem difficult or undesirable as a customer.

Advertising Your Grape Provider

I suggest as a good practice to indicate the vineyard of origin on your varietal wine labels. TTB rules do not permit a winery to use an American Viticultural Area (AVA) name on a label if the winery and the grower are in different states. I was in Idaho and my fruit came from Washington. To get around this regulation and still credit my grower's vineyard required a little bit of cunning. TTB rules allowed me to label my wine as "Washington grown" and name the vineyard, as long as I didn't mention the AVA. This labeling practice allowed me to credit the grower, which was good for them as I regularly won commercial awards for my wines.

Trading off a Small Cost for Big Labor Savings

I sometimes bought juice rather than whole grapes. If a grower was also a winery, they had the ability to sell fresh clarified juice. The usual cost to have grapes converted to juice was $50 per ton. Do the math—150 gallons of wine per ton, 5 bottles per gallon, translates to $0.07 per bottle extra cost. Not too bad.

Not having to crush and press the fruit saved wear-and-tear on my body because, outside of the tasting room, I had no regular staff to help crush grapes for the five to six thousand gallons of wine I made per year. Your body is a precious resource when you're operating a small winery. Hurting your back, elbow, shoulder, or knee can result in both physical and financial pain. The $0.07 per bottle to have my grapes crushed was a good cost trade-off for my not seeing a chiropractor and not using prescription anti-inflammatories. Oh yes, and less pain!

Conclusions

You only get one chance to sell a bad bottle of wine or a bad anything else to someone. Do not squander the advertising money already spend to develop a customer. Production quality may not be the place to scrimp. Unless you are choosing a market spot based solely on retail price, be very careful about lowering the quality of your raw materials.

46.   Selling the Business

General business points:
- **Preparing your business for sale**
- **Equipment value**
- **Blue sky**
- **Selling price**

In the first chapter of this book I discussed the history of Camas Winery. By 1999, I had retired from the Feds. In 2003, I also retired from the Army Reserve. By 2004, Camas Prairie was the oldest independent winery in North Idaho. Sales were stronger than ever. We sold 1,900 cases in 2004. By the time I sold the business in 2011, net profits had doubled from 2004 levels and we had two employees in the tasting room. Not bad for a hobby run amok. Life is pleasant and I continue to not just learn fast, but to learn good! It seems to be working.

The Harvesting Phase

In 2008, I entered the harvesting stage of business. In this phase the operation is polished for future sale. Information on sources, practices, and procedures that has long been in my head was transcribed. Much as a franchise operation provides new owners with how-to manuals, our own practices and lessons learned were put into written form to help sell the business and assist the future operator. In January 2011, the winery operation sold to a young couple.

When you create a business, somewhere in your mind should be the realization that at some point, you want to have a saleable operation. Along those lines, here are a few things to keep in mind as you grow your business.

Setting the Price

When it comes time to sell your winery, the buyer will probably need a little help. Banks will usually loan on the value of the hard assets and not the blue sky portion of the sale price. That means the value of your hard assets must be determined. I helped the bank, the buyer, and myself by establishing the value of the equipment in my winery.

Equipment valuation

Unlike buying or selling a used car, there is no blue book for used winery equipment. Working from the county tax assessor's spreadsheet of winery equipment, I set about determining the current replacement value of each item. Sometimes the value of a particular piece of equipment could be established by an Internet search. Other times, I had the original vendor send me a written quote to establish an item's replacement cost. In the end I had a file of documents that independently established the value of all my equipment if it were to be purchased new. From this aggregated replacement-value figure, the lender was then free to establish what they considered the actual value of the collateral based on a percentage of the replacement cost.

This approach had credibility for both the bank and buyer. Neither entity had to accept what might have been a self-serving estimate of equipment values. In my particular case, the bank set the value of the equipment at fifty percent of the current replacement cost.

Blue Sky Assets

Financial institutions only make loans on the value of tangible objects such as equipment and inventory. But of course, you will have a little bit of blue sky in your sale price.

Blue sky is the value of such things as your client list, supplier list, distribution network, trademarks, service marks, labels, formulas, website, mailing list, and anything else you might term as goodwill and reputation. Many of these items cost you real-world dollars. It costs money to have labels created by an artist, to have printer's proofs or foil dies made, and to obtain label and formula approvals. There are fees associated with registering trademarks and service marks with the various states and the Federal Government. You'll spend time and money on samples and travel expenses to develop your clients and your distribution network. Website designs and entry fees for wine competitions require large sums of money. While not part of your tangible assets, blue sky items are expensive!

The sad truth is that all of these blue sky elements are invisible to the bank for purposes of securing a loan. This means a potential buyer must have available funds of his own. No bank will loan 100% of your desired sale price if you have blue sky elements figured into that price.

Also, keep in mind that paying capital gains tax is a very real cost when profiting from the sale of your business. And, just to make things more complicated, equipment and inventory are taxed at a different rate than the value of the blue sky elements that you include in your sale price.

The resulting price

Using the bank's assessment as a model, I based my asking price on fifty percent of the replacement cost for my equipment, furniture, and fixtures. I added to this my valuation of the blue sky, which was demonstrated by approved labels, formulas, trademarks, five years of tax returns, and my client lists for wholesale and retail customers. The bank and buyer also got annual sales figures broken down by category: wine retail, wine wholesale, beer, accessories, food, custom labeling and catering. I kept the blue sky value low because that was the portion of the asking price that banks would not lend against, so it would represent "skin-in-the-game" for the buyer. Using this formula, I was able to establish a basis for my asking price that was not merely pulled out of thin air or based on my own ego.

Conclusions

Selling your business is in many ways analogous to selling your house. We begin by making it saleable; painting, fixing little things and choosing how we plan to sell. We might select a realtor to market the property or choose to sell it ourselves. Central to either sales mode is setting a realistic asking price. In residential property we use "comps" to guide us in settling on a price. In the following chapters I'll talk about the business equivalent activities that are akin to "comps." The other component of the price will be your view of the intangibles, or blue sky elements. In a residential context "blue sky" equates to the quality of the local schools, the neighborhood, and access to goods, services, entertainment and recreation.

Be able to explain your asking price and its component parts on a clear, factual and reasoned basis. Doing so will help you fine-tune the price to be realistic for the buyer. Remember the buyer usually will need financing so you want to help them have a good basis for getting bank assistance. The bank will set its own value on your equipment and real estate. You and the buyer will be well served by knowing the replacement value of everything that is being offered for sale.

47. Helping the Buyer

General business points:
- **Creating purchasing options**
- **Carrying back a note**
- **Stealing ideas from franchises**
- **Consulting**

You may be selling to Warren Buffett, Jeff Bezos, or Donald Trump; if so, tell me how you did it! If you are selling to someone who needs financing, whatever the source, help them make a credible presentation that would justify granting a loan. The buyer must show the lender that the assets of the business collateralize the loan principal. Also the buyer must show that the business cash flow is sufficient to service the loan, meet the overhead, and still show a profit. Without all of these three elements covered, the loan will not be approved.

The biggest risk in applying for a loan is allowing the lender to think that you have not done your homework regarding the two-way cash flow that is involved with any business. Lenders want to loan money because that's how they make money. That said, lenders do loans for a living and will know in a hot minute if you are a worthy, serious, candidate who deserves their assumption of risk. Banks hate risk so you must show that their loan is well capitalized.

So help the buyer meet these three thresholds by having:
- A comprehensive listing of all equipment with each item's current replacement cost
- A minimum of three years of business tax returns
- An itemized accounting of overhead expenses, customer list and current list of debts and receivables

Creating Purchase Options for a Buyer

Alerting potential buyers to their options seemed to soften the shock of how complex the winery business can be. About two years before the actual sale of the winery I wrote a specific outline of sales options, which I will call the "purchase options offering sheet." I then reviewed the options with my real estate agents so they were clear on the options and prices that were offered for sale. My offering sheet had four sections:

- Buying the business and equipment
- Buying the inventory (see options below)
- Renting the premises
- Hiring me as a consulting winemaker to insure continuity of the product

I also laid out a plan to show potential buyers how they could transition from my business model of producing all of my own wines to the alternative models of buying bulk wines to bottle and sell. I also explained the option of a BYOB program and described how each of these models can be mixed—BYOB, make some of your wines while buying and bottling others, etc.

Buying the business

This was the first section of the purchase options offering sheet. The business was the primary item being offered for sale, and as such was not negotiable, except in price. What I mean by non-negotiable is that the other items related to the winery, as outlined in numbers 2 through 4 of the offering sheet, were purchasable as an option.

Inventory

Inventory can be a little tricky when it comes to selling a business. To help me with my preparations, I found a realtor in California who specialized in winery acquisitions. I asked this realtor if it was better for me to sell down the inventory, so the sale price would be lower for a buyer, or better for me to have a robust inventory at the time of sale.

The consultant advised that if the winery is being sold because it is failing, then you want the smallest inventory possible. If the winery is successful and being sold due to retirement (as was my case), then you want to offer a healthy inventory.

The consultant did advise that even in the scenario of selling a successful business, you should do one more thing to the inventory. Before offering the business for sale, prune the slowest-selling items from the product line and inventory. Slow-selling items, no matter how good, are a drag on the inventory because of the space they occupy and the UCAP tax obligation they constantly accumulate.

Taking this advice to heart, I discontinued three items: a North African-style honey wine, a sweet red dessert wine, and a dry red sparkling wine. These wines had earned awards in wine competitions, but they were difficult to sell. The common element causing the sluggish sales of these special wines was their unique nature. At the tasting room, a customer could try these wines with no risk, but in retail stores, their exotic nature was a little intimidating. This meant they had to go.

After we had pruned the three slow sellers, the inventory portion of the purchase offering was divided into two components, each of which the eventual buyer could choose to purchase along with the business. These two components were purchase choices—wines and beer only or complete inventory including accessories—and gave the buyer options that could be exercised in accordance with his budget and business plan.

Of course, inventories fluctuate on an almost daily basis so we avoided setting a specific value of inventory on the offering sheet. Instead, we specified that whichever portion of the inventory was being purchased would be valued at wholesale or wine production cost, and by a physical inventory at closing.

The main issue with our inventory, as an item in the sale of the business, occurred in part due to the sequence of events during the sale. Because the inventory was as yet unvalued, the buyer was forced to place a guestimate dollar amount on the inventory in his written offer. The offer, once accepted, became an important document in the bank's review of the loan application. Both events—guestimate and loan application—took place prior to a completed inventory being prepared at closing. This meant we had to reassure the bank that the value of the inventory exceeded the dollar amount on the offer. We had to find a way for the buyer to pay the difference between the bank loan and the true value of the inventory, at closing, if a difference existed.

To satisfy the bank, we performed an inventory of the bulk wines. This quick-and-dirty procedure substantiated the value of the inventory as exceeding the amount of money necessary to cover the money loaned to the buyer. With the bank's immediate concern resolved, we now needed to get me paid for the value of any extra inventory that might be on premises at the time the business changed ownership.

We managed this accommodation by creating a separate note for the buyer to pay the difference on the value of the inventory. The amount of this promissory note would be the difference between the amount in the offer we had accepted and the inventory value as determined by the physical inventory at close of escrow. It all worked out well in the end.

Selling your business can be separate from selling your location or other real estate.

The third section of the purchase options offering sheet concerned the renting of the winery space. Since I owned the building where I operated my winery, a buyer could choose to rent the winery space from me or to move the business to a new location. To prepare this section of the purchase options, I obtained a commercial appraisal of my building to use when determining the fair market value of the rental space. The total space offered for rent had four specific areas: tasting room and wine bar loft, wine storage area, production area, and dry warehouse storage. I chose to take the appraised values of the winery space in its several parts and offer the entire area at ten percent below fair market value, which gave the buyer an economic incentive to stay as my tenant. The option sheet also allowed the buyer to rent a smaller area at a lower rent price. Since I lived above the business, my family would fill in any unused space.

My motivation for adopting the strategy of possibly renting a smaller area to the buyer was based on a long-term perspective. As a landlord, my greatest risk is having a vacant building, and my long-term finances are potentially linked to my tenant's success. Many businesses have failed because their overhead costs were too high, so I created options for the buyer, even if that might mean a portion of my space went unrented.

By eliminating the need for a buyer to rent all of the space previously used, I opened up the sale of my business to a variety of business models. For example, the buyer might have a business plan that focused on enhanced food service. To do this, a buyer would need to add a restaurant kitchen. This would require them to take space from another winery activity, such as the production area for the sparkling wine or a subsection of the wine product area. It was also possible that a buyer might choose to use a mobile bottling line or even to buy their wines instead of making their own. Other business models were now possible because the buyer held the option of renting only the space he needed.

Consultant services: supporting your buyer after the sale

After-sale support of your buyer goes a long way to reducing the chance that they will default on any note that you had to carry back as part of the contract of sale. The final section of the purchase options offering sheet concerned my willingness to work for a year as a consulting winemaker for a bargain rate of $10 per hour. Once again, this was an option for the buyer and not a required element of the sale.

To prepare this option, I had an attorney create a consultant services contract that I could customize as needed. The consultant option was calculated to give continuity to the product line and to ease the buyer into the business without alarming the public or commercial accounts about changes to the products. Perception is reality, so if a customer mistakenly believed a change in ownership meant a change in the quality of wines, then the winery's reputation would be diminished. Secondly, my buyer might take comfort in knowing that he could call on me to answer the inevitable questions that arise after purchasing an existing business.

In summary, I tried to create purchase options that were clear and supported the buyer's efforts while recognizing that their vision of the winery could be different from mine. The options were built upon the idea that selling a business is not like a war where you have a winner and a loser. If done properly, the sale should produce two winners since I believed that my economic future and the buyer's economic future were linked.

Carrying Back a Note

I also helped all parties in the transaction by deciding in advance what amount of the sale price I was willing and able to carry on a promissory note. I shared this information with my realtor, but we did not disclose this information to the buyer. My ability to help by taking back a promissory note was intended to assist the buyer with the blue sky and possibly inventory portions of the purchase price.

The face value of a promissory note is money you will still have at risk after the sale of your business. Your note can't be secured by the same collateral that has been pledged to the bank. My note was not secured by the liquid inventory. It was essentially an unsecured note, so my money was still at risk.

This being an imperfect world, my willingness to participate in financing the purchase was necessary. My point here is to acquaint you with a bank's inability to loan on the blue sky in the sale price and to explain how I helped my buyer by considering in advance what help I would be willing to offer. To incentivize the buyer's paying off the unsecured note I included the following. The note would be for a period of five years at an interest rate of 3%, with equal payments due on the first of each month. Each 12 months, if every payment had been on time and in full, the balance on the note would be reduced by an extra 5%.

Offering Some of the Supportive Aspects of a *Franchise*

I learned while lecturing at the University of Idaho why the business model of franchises was so appealing to folks who wanted to start or buy into the business world. Basically, a franchise is a package where you get equipment and training as a package deal from the seller of the franchise. While I was not able to offer all the appeal and support of a franchise opportunity

185

with a national brand, I could adapt some of their points to the sale of my winery.

When it came time to sell the business, a copy of my training and procedure manual and other related personnel forms were shown to potential buyers. Also provided were the personnel forms I created that included a basic contract with the employee that specified hours/days of work, rate of pay, allowable vacation periods, and grounds for termination.

Conclusions

Prepare the business for sale by creating everything that will help a buyer: procedure manuals, training manuals, customer and supplier lists. Anything that will reduce the elements that make buyers apprehensive is to your advantage.

If any substantial portion of your asking price is based on the "blue sky" elements of an existing customer base, sales and earnings history and reputation, be cautious. If you carry a contract of sale for all or part of the asking price, you risk getting back a failed business with no customers, no cash flow, and a damaged or outright bad reputation. Being "the bank" is extremely risky.

48. Stu's Ten Commandments:

1. Learn the Excel spread sheet program.
2. Take a simple bookkeeping class.
3. Join your local Chamber of Commerce.
4. Take every opportunity to speak to groups or classes as free advertising.
5. Buying grapes may be easier and smarter than growing grapes.
6. Learn some Spanish.
7. Always make a small donation to local charities whenever asked.
8. Many small adjustments are preferable to a few big changes.
9. We are never as smart as we think we are; smile more, bitch less.
10. Don't ask for an item's price. Ask for its delivered price.

Conclusion

Now you know what I did, what I learned and what I survived during my 28 years in the wine business. The lessons learned were business lessons, most of which are not unique to the wine business. Here's hoping that the concepts presented are clear and will help you along your own chosen path. Happy trails!

Stu

The End

About the Author

After returning from the Air Force, Stu Scott worked as staff in a juvenile detention facility, moving on to adult probation and finally to federal probation and parole. Simultaneously, in 1980 he returned to the military as a reserve agent with the Army Criminal Investigation Command. Born and raised in the San Francisco bay area, he has lived with his wife in Moscow, Idaho since 1981. Believing that we only go around once in life and that one job is never enough, his other careers include: professional winemaker, college instructor, director of a school for disabled children and stained glass artist.

Comments or questions for Stu?

sls@turbonet.com

Also By This Author

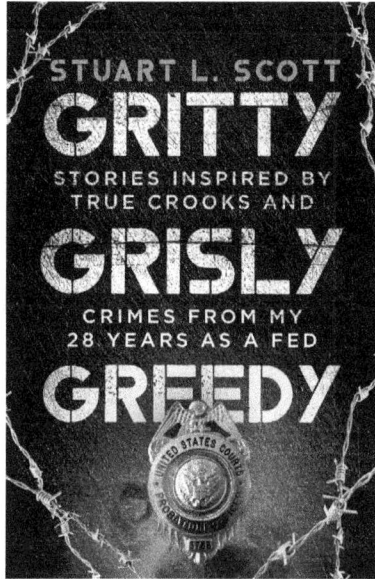

The Tooth Fairy
A story as cold as a Spokane winter about what happens
when a crook chooses the wrong victim.
The Grand Tetons
The Texas bank robber who carries twin 38's.
Idaho Catch and Release
Husband and wife pornographers who give a new
meaning to what's really a crime.
The Deal
The 1976 case of a crooked politician revisited in 2016.
Available at Amazon in paperback and on Kindle
ISBN:978-1-7322468-1-2

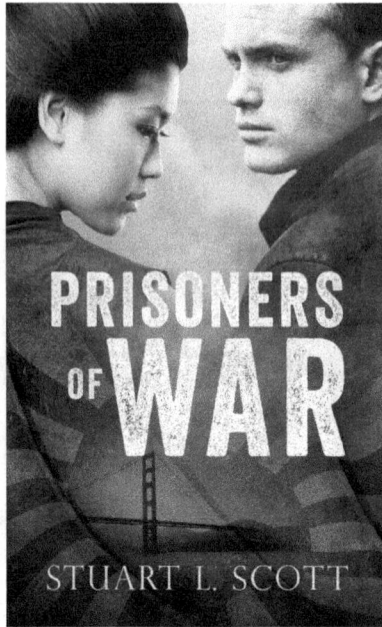

Prisoners of War is simultaneously a love story, a mystery and a history, all woven together. Everything of a historical nature is true to the best of my knowledge and research. Conflict between love and duty. Conflict between love of country and the love of your life. How far would you go to win back your love, when the government has taken her away? Fear, racism and abiding love collide in 1942 America, when your only crime was being born Japanese.

Available at Amazon in paperback and on Kindle

ISBN: 978-1-7322468-2-9